the Cost of our Lives

Do you have the patience to wait
Until the mud settles and the water is clear?
Can you remain unmoving
Until the right action arises by itself?

—Lao Tzu

the Cost of our Lives

Linda González

E.L. Marker
Salt Lake City

Published by E.L. Marker, an imprint of WiDo Publishing

WiDō Publishing
Salt Lake City, Utah
widopublishing.com

Cover design by Steven Novak
Book design by Marny K. Parkin

ISBN: 978-1-937178-97-0

Printed in the United States of America

Contents

For my cuates Gina y Teotli,
who grew up as this story matured
and always give me the ganas to go the long, hard
way
with love and compassion

Part 1:
Flight

My parents Rosendo and Isabel in Los Ángeles, 1955

Holiday picture in our second home
with my mom's tía Lucrecia and Gloria, 1961

1.
We Can Never Go Back

I DON'T REMEMBER A SINGLE DETAIL OF THE DAY I
met my brother Miguel. None of my siblings remember
either, but given what had happened before ese día and
what followed in the years after, what occurred is easy to
imagine.

When the doorbell rings that late afternoon in 1974, I
jump, almost in sync with my sister Susan. We are lying
down, our noses buried in books. Our dark eyes devour
the words that send us away to a world of stories that
cradle our tender hearts. I am reading the latest Agatha
Christie mystery, a collection of Hercule Poirot's early
cases. He is an unlikely hero for a sixteen year old, especially since I don't share his fastidious nature. Scotland
Yard underrates him because of his foppish looks and
thick accent, and yet, he always catches the bad guys, the
only attribute that matters for a detective.

When the door opens, so will the first of many secrets
that crack our familia apart over the years, giving way to
the liquid mantle layer underneath tectonic plates. Everything moves below the quiet crust until the plates crash
into and rub against each other. These often silent and
jarring interactions do serious damage over time. Two
voices insinuate themselves into my head. One is my

father's—curt and low. The other is expansive and rapid-fire; it must be Miguel.

A kitchen cupboard slams hard, and I jump again. My mom is in the kitchen, just off our bedroom. She says something in a low growl and then the refrigerator door bangs shut. Her heels click along the linoleum to the sink, and water rushes out of the tap as if she is deliberately drowning the voices that stop in our living room. I imagine my father and Miguel sitting on the shiny turquoise-flecked couch. The fireplace is not lit because of the balmy fall weather.

"Niños. Isabel." My dad commands us to emerge from the safety of our bedrooms. This scene feels similar, but the memory is lost in the dark shadows accumulating in my mind. My sister, a bit over a year older than me, rises to a seated position. Susan's shag haircut frames her book and her shoulders hunch forward. I worked hard this morning to straighten my tight curls and envy her wavy hair. Sliding my feet onto the rug, I reluctantly place the bookmark into the thick of my unsolved mystery.

"Come on!" I say.

I don't want to go out alone, don't want to push down the fear clogging my chest from all the times I have been called out to meet someone who speaks Spanish and disrupts my life. Susan moves like the afternoon sun across our backyard, no rush at all to arrive at the scene unfolding in our living room.

Our younger brother, Eddy, is matching her turtle speed in his adjoining bedroom, the one he shared with our abuela, Conchita, before she died a few years back. He might be reading or he might be constructing elaborate battle scenes with his army of small plastic soldiers.

Sometimes I sneak a peek from the hallway and watch as he makes soft gun noises beside a soldier holding a rifle on the windowsill. He then knocks down the soldier who was killed. The soldier next to his fallen mate returns fire, killing the man who shot his buddy. His wars are so orderly. Sometimes he emerges from the room armed with his combat helmet and rifle, ready to do battle on his belly in front of the TV.

"So tranquilo, ever since he was born," my mom often says.

Now she is anything but tranquila, as her heels continue their staccato rhythm from stove to sink to refrigerator, but not toward the men's voices.

"Niños!"

Again, more tersely, my father calls us, leaving his wife out. He must be hearing what we hear, knowing she will not be so easily led.

I walk down the hallway towards the living room. As I turn the corner, I hear my mom stirring the steaming frijoles with a spoon, imagine her left hand in a fist by her side, her full red lips pursed.

Susan and Eddy are behind me as I grudgingly enter the living room.

My father wears his own thin-lipped smile incongruent with eyes empty of mirth. He is neither stocky nor slender, and his hair is combed back so that his tight dark curls, like mine, are flattened out.

"Te presento a tu hermano, Miguel."

Another crash. This time it is the oven door.

Even though our father has told us this man, our brother, is coming to dinner, seeing Miguel doesn't make it feel real. I shove my anxiety down into my stomach.

"Hola," I say. I want the day to end so I can get back to my book and my bed.

Miguel is lean and about the same height as my dad, not much over five-six, and they share almond-shaped eyes. His smile is wide, and he bounds over to me like a Golden Retriever puppy eager to be petted.

I reach out a hand, which Miguel grabs to pull me into a hug, his brightly colored shirt cool against me. His pants are polyester and flared at the bottom, and his shoes are brown and pointy. He looks as if he has won the lottery, and we look like we have lost. Miguel's hair is lighter than any of ours and wavy like Susan's. Miguel walks over to Eddy, who had thought he was the only hijo of the familia, the Rosendo Jr. of the clan, and hugs him, too.

Eddy is as stiff as I was. I can't read anything on his face. He pushes his glasses further up his nose and rocks from one foot to another. Miguel's energy makes the dim emotional lights of our family flicker in panic.

Then Miguel turns and hugs Susan. Like a cat in a showdown with a dog, her pupils narrow and she pulls her head back. Her gaze moves to my dad, and she blinks several times as if trying not to cry, as if somebody has just hit her in the stomach and she can't breathe. She stumbles backwards after Miguel releases her and grabs the edge of the laminate wood entertainment center, her eyes still on Tot. She gave our father this nickname many years earlier, and that is what we call him. Never Dad, never Papi.

Susan keeps her arms tightly crossed, disappearing into an inner cave where no one is allowed. She remembers this moment being very straightforward. *He's your brother.* She begins to have an image of Tot that is different than before, like when a mirror breaks. Even if you piece it back together, the cracks remain. For her, the blow comes from Tot, not Miguel. As the oldest, she sees more meaning than I do in this meeting. Susan is no longer the oldest.

"It's okay, you guys," says Miguel. "I speak some English. I have been here for one half years."

Does he mean one and a half years, or half a year? Tot shoots him a look that says "Cállate," and the light in Miguel's eyes darkens. He takes a breath as if to fill himself up with courage and ignores my father's look.

"Nice yard." Miguel tries again, motioning with one of his hands towards the big sliding glass doors that open onto our large backyard. The grass is green from early rain, and a few sparrows are flicking water off their wings in the birdbath. The plum, peach, and apricot trees have no leaves. They sway in the breeze that is bringing in a thin layer of fog from Venice Beach a few miles away. I wish I was there now, instead of in this house full of people holding their breath.

We all jump at another crash from the kitchen. My mom must have dropped a serving platter. She is a key actor in this scene even if she remains off-stage, cursing the god who keeps tearing the canvas of the family portrait she has painted. We move cautiously into the kitchen and sit down around the oval table. Susan and I have already set out placemats, forks, glasses, and plates. The early evening sun casts small lines through the shades on the sliding glass doors.

"Sit down." My mom's voice slides out of the back of her throat and around the short, brown waves of her hair. She is not even pretending to be a gracious hostess; her hostility is as thick as her accent when she speaks English.

I am usually the most reluctant hostess, mumbling my "Holas" and slinking into my bedroom as soon as the adults get caught up in their conversation and forget I am there. All three of us have read a hell of a lot of books over the years —crowding out the Spanish we hear our parents and their friends speak through closed doors.

"Susan!" My mom's voice interrupts the awkward silence. "Heat up the tortillas."

Susan scurries up, only too happy to pull the bag out of the refrigerator and join my mother at the stove. Their frames match up, both slightly over five feet, but Susan has inherited my father's darker complexion in contrast to my mom's creamy skin.

Still as statues, we wait, hands pressed down on our laps. My mom approaches the table with a rectangular Pyrex full of hot enchiladas, the cheese still bubbling. She abandoned much of her Colombian cuisine when she married my dad. Miguel rises instinctively, and she nods, her eyes narrowing, willing him to die. This look has scalded me many times when I refuse to toe her line, but today it is burning hotter. She is not going to accept one of those huge abrazos, not going to make this intruder comfortable in her home.

Mom is known for her efficiency at the business office job at Kaiser, and that is her approach at home. Susan skirts around her and lays down the folded cloth nestling our daily ration of corn tortillas.

"Linda. The ensalada."

"And the chiles."

Tot's voice follows on the heels of my mom's; the war between them escalating, nearing ground zero where there are no winners. Never, ever, do I see sadness or fear from my father or mother. Instead, they have overused anger since exiting US customs and they are doing so again today.

I squeeze past Susan. Picking up the white bowl with hand-painted radishes and carrots, I am glad to see avocado from our tree sliced in with the iceberg lettuce and tomatoes. That, and lots of Thousand Island dressing will make the salad and dinner conversation tolerable.

Miguel's left hand is clenched, lying on the table. His fury is leaking out from behind the smile plastered on his face as he sees what he lost at age seven, when my dad left him almost twenty years before. No more delusion, no more thinning out the pain of his childhood. Unlike my mom, he tempers his rage, his chest rising and falling in one big sigh.

Why are you here? I want to yell. *And what do you want?*

"So, you all play fútbol?" he asks, turning towards where I sit between Susan and Eddy.

There is no pretending either of them will answer. And I can't bear the quiet. If anyone will say something, it has to be me, the most unimportant pawn in this game, the one who could rival Miguel's exuberance.

"We play soccer, if that's what you mean. I thought about joining my high school team, but . . ." Oh, boy. I am saying too much. I serve myself salad and pass it to my sister.

"That's great," Miguel replies.

"En los estados unidos," my dad's voice has the sharp edge he unsheathes to slay someone's ideas, "they *let* the girls play. Not like en México."

What is he doing? He brings this man to our house, this brother, which means his son, and then he switches sides in the middle of the game. For a split second, I feel sorry for Miguel.

"Do you want some?" I say to him, offering the enchiladas.

"*Quieres* se murió." Tot's voice spits out one of his dichos. In his house, we don't ask if people want food, we just give it. It is his idea of hospitality.

My mom sits down and keeps the food moving into her mouth as if daring anyone to talk to her. Our house stinks of shame and fear, as if dead rats under the floorboards have reached the worst stage of decomposition and all you want to do is get as far away as possible and let someone else clean up the rotten remains.

We must have stumbled through dinner. My dad might have taken Miguel to the backyard to look for avocados on our two large trees. We girls likely washed and dried the dishes. Eddy would have gone to his room. And mom must have gone to their room, no *adiós* or *I hate you* necessary. Her bedroom door slamming says it all.

Later, after the house is quiet again, I think about my mom's unspoken tantrum. I hear the rise and fall of my parents' Spanish floating down the hallway to our magenta bedroom in the back of the house we have lived in since I was seven years old. Because my father works mostly evenings and weekends at the Century Plaza hotel as a banquet captain, he and my mom chose the smaller front bedroom with a half bathroom that leads to the garage. That way, he parks his car and enters the house without disturbing anyone.

Their conversations often soothe me to sleep, but tonight the tones are sharp, like spears seeking the chinks in armor. They do not give ground without a fight, preferring direct attacks, unlike the controlled war today. Mom is not the housewife a sus órdenes kind of mujer. She is the one to exact a price, because no child of Tot's will call him out.

Their voices become lower and lower, and my eyelids droop with the exhaustion of navigating shaky ground. A line has been crossed, and we can never go back to before the doorbell rang. My mom will make sure of that. Miguel will, too. On that they are oddly joined. I didn't realize it then, but I lost my relationship with the word *love* that day. It became a wisp of what it had been, or maybe it had never really existed.

Sin decir nada, Susan and I agree on how to get our ducks back in their rows after Miguel's arrival by pretending the dinner and he are no big deal. It helps that Miguel rarely comes to visit for the next few years as he settles into his life in Los Angeles.

By the time he starts dropping by the house more frequently, I am living at college. Susan—who understands our family life has a crack that can only get bigger—keeps her heart tentatively open to Miguel. She remembers him living alone in an apartment and being very much on his own. She recalls Tot meeting him away from the house, and she also makes a point to see him periodically. We have not yet discovered all the stars in our family constellation, and I don't yet care about how this all came to be.

2.
Uniting el Cielo con la Tierra

I TOOK AN ORAL HISTORY CLASS IN MY THIRD YEAR of college and decided to interview my parents about how they came to the United States. During the Christmas holiday break, my mom and I settled on the couch with the tape recorder between us.

Linda: We're in the home of Mr. and Mrs. González. This is Linda González, student, taping an interview with Isabel González, my mother. So let's begin. Just talk normal. Vamos a hacerlo en inglés o español?

Isabel: What would be better for you? Are you going to translate this?

L: No. I just have to write a paper on it. Not so much what you said. I might transcribe it, but I may not.

I: Can you understand if I say it in Spanish?

L: Yes! *(annoyed tone)*

I: Okay, then do it in Spanish.

Mi mamita, Isabel, was also known as Chava and was born in 1924 in Anolaima, a small town in Colombia. I already knew she was la del medio, with an older brother, Luis, and a younger sister, Marina. When her mother, Maria Josefa, died in childbirth, she was sent with her siblings to live with her father Pablo's sisters in a pueblo far from her birth town, at the age of two.

At age six, she was sent alone to Bogotá to live with her maternal tía Lucrecia and my mom's abuela. When I asked her whether she wanted to leave her siblings and her paternal tías, she said, "I don't know if I wanted to go or not, and they didn't ask me, they just sent me. Ju know."

That "ju know" is so touching, as if I had any idea what it would be like for a two-year-old girl to lose her parents and be sent to a passel of tías on a farm for four years, and then lose her siblings in a move to a big city.

In Bogotá, she was kept inside a house instead of running free on a farm. Not surprisingly, she became ill, and the doctor's astute diagnosis was that the change had impacted her physical health. My mom recounts this as if saying the sky is blue, as if she were not a sad six-year-old trying to adjust to her third home, bereft of parents, siblings, and the broad landscape of the campo. His prescription was to take her outdoors, because she was used to being "al aire libre" and needed to play with girls her age.

For five long years, she remained alone with her tía and abuela, creating her own entertainment in a stern household, until her brother and sister came to live with her when she was eleven. My mom always referred to her mother's sister, Lucrecia, as mi tía, and so I thought her name was Mitía.

"Mitía wanted us to be educated, to go to college." Her aunt was in her fifties, her hair already white and her family's financial assets in a state of decline. My mom's abuela disagreed with Mitía's decision to raise her sister's children, saying in front of them that they were a burden. Chava and her siblings retaliated by doing what they knew would annoy their abuela, like making a racket when she was napping and stepping in mud so they could leave dirty footprints in her house.

Mitía also took in another child, who was raised as a much younger sibling of Chava. Gloria, who has been connected to my mother and us all her life, confirmed my mother's sense that Mitía supported herself through her friends. Chava's maternal family was very well connected and used to belong to prestigious circles with people close to the president, until her family earnings turned sour.

Mitía no longer worked. Chava was the most level-headed and also the most stubborn, according to Gloria. If you said to sit down, she would say, "No, I will stand." If someone said green, my mom said yellow. Gloria called it la ley contrario al pueblo, and I had seen it in my mom all my life. There are some in my family who would say I inherited that from her.

There was no one shepherding Chava into her adolescence, no one encouraging her to fly and providing a cushion if she fell. She landed in a boarding school for three years of high school when Mitía found a scholarship for her. There was something in my mom that always rebelled, the middle child searching for her place, unable to sit still, what is now called a spirited child. She left the classroom when teachers told her not to and teased other girls in class until they laughed—"de payasa."

Clowning around was a strategy she carried with her until she died. When I asked her how often she was deprived of field trips and home visits for breaking the rules, she admitted with a laugh: "Almost all the time."

After graduating, she started a college business program. She hated not having what she needed, embarrassed by her dependence on her tía's friends. She quit school to work, leaving Bogotá to live with some cousins an hour away.

Mitía didn't like either of these choices, pushing her to be a teacher and return home. In the coming years, my mom dabbled in professions without the benefit of a formal education, relying instead on her clever mind, quick wit, and capacity to smile as if she had been loved well.

As a teacher, she did not play favorites, and her actions were based on standards that did not waver in the face of opposition. Nowhere is this more evident than a story she shared about a boy she taught. They took the kids to Catholic mass every Sunday. One student arrived bathed and with a clean shirt, but barefoot. To attend mass, they all had to wear shoes or sandals. The principal told him, "You can't go to mass; stay here."

Chava said, "No, he goes to mass. He is clean, and not having shoes is not his fault. What is the law that says you can't go to mass barefoot? He goes."

The principal did not expect her, a young teacher, to challenge him in front of everyone. Because they respected each other as colleagues, he swallowed his anger, let the child attend mass, and did not reprimand her. I like to think he knew she was right. Pride beamed from her face as she finished her cuento.

Chava was restless and itching for more of a challenge, so she returned to Bogotá after two years. Mitía refused to help her get a job because my mom continued to make decisions without accepting consejos. Undeterred by her aunt's disapproval, she contacted a doctor whose son she had taught. Because she had eliminated his son's stutter and helped him read, he had given her his card. The doctor used his connections to secure her a job at a bank. Once again she had no training, but a friend of Mitía's worked there and covered for her while she learned her duties. She wore the mask of competence until she had indeed achieved it.

This pattern of constantly having to pretend reinforced her underlying insecurity. She never appreciated her ability to assimilate information and think on her feet. Her belief she was less important than others had soaked into her groundwater despite her outward panache. Chava developed a warm friendship at the bank with Alicia, who eventually moved to the US and pestered my mom to join her. Chava was disconsolate living with Mitía, her younger sister Marina, and Gloria. She worked hard and paid the rent and almost all the bills.

As the months passed, Alicia's invitation to come to the US became more and more appealing. The final straw may have been the political atmosphere in Colombia. It was becoming un poco feo. The guerrilleros had increased their attacks because their leader, Gaitán, had been assassinated. The pueblo rose up, as they loved him, looting stores and burning buildings with gasoline bombs.

One day, my mom stumbled onto a rally in front of the Palace of the President on her way to lunch at a cousin's house. She couldn't go home to her Chápinero neighborhood and had no way to tell Mitía. After a few days people were allowed to leave the city, but only by displaying a permit to heavily armed soldiers. A state of civil war was declared, with a curfew of eight o'clock imposed for three months.

This political turmoil drove Chava to enlist Alicia's assistance in beginning her emigration process. Alicia excitedly walked her through the affidavit procedures. A

US citizen named Smith sent it to Chava, and she took it to the embassy.

The consular officer asked why Mr. Smith gave Chava the affidavit. My mom laughed as she told me she quickly made up a story, telling them her father had often traveled and had lived in Barranquilla, where many people visited because of the coastal climate and tourist attractions. He had met Mr. Smith there and they had become good friends. Mr. Smith had told him if he or his family ever wanted to travel to the United States he would help them. She told the officer she didn't remember him because she was very young at the time, but her father had talked about Mr. Smith with cariño. The officials believed her and my mom had conned yet another authority figure.

Mitía and her siblings were not happy about her decision, but her friends were jealous, believing that coming to the United States was to unite el cielo con la tierra. She immigrated in 1951, at the beginning of a period labeled La Violencia, when hundreds of thousands were killed or displaced. She was part of the first year of a fifty-year migration spike, making Colombians the largest South American immigrant group in the United States.

❧

My mom's very first plane ride to Los Angeles was five hours long. She didn't know anyone except Alicia, and she did not speak English. She stayed with Alicia's friend, Doris. After a few visits, Alicia inexplicably quit calling or coming to the house. After a year had passed with no word, my mom decided to go to Alicia's apartment.

She wanted to surprise Alicia and asked David, Doris's husband, to take her. She still held tightly to her dream to live with Alicia and enjoy herself. This was an opportunity to have fun as a young woman in her mid-twenties. David warned her that she should not expect to find the friend she had known, because people changed when they came to the US. He left her at the front of a shabby apartment building, saying he would return in an hour. Instead, he parked close by, waiting to see what happened.

My mom knocked, and Alicia opened the door, looking surprised but not pleased. Instead of inviting her in, Alicia asked how Chava had found her. She said she was leaving soon, gave Chava her phone number, and abruptly closed the door. My mom stood there for a few minutes, unable to believe her one friend had closed the door on her like she was a nuisance.

While she sat dejectedly in the passenger seat, David laughed and said: "I told you people change. You expected to find the Alicia you knew in Colombia, and she didn't even let you in."

In bed that night, I imagine my mom engulfed with questions that had no answers, loss that felt all too familiar. What was Alicia hiding? My mom never called her or tried to visit Alicia again, unable to get over the look on her face and her own heartbreaking disappointment.

My mom nonetheless was determined to make Los Angeles her home. She first found work as a house cleaner and then in factories. She itched to be free of David and Doris, who resented the time she spent with friends, as they wanted her to be available to watch their two sons. My mom had left Colombia to escape family obligations, and she found herself back in the same pattern.

She also disliked David's attempts to set her up with an older friend of his, who would visit often. More annoyingly, this man was often waiting outside her work to take her home. He offered her everything to marry him. He owned his house and other properties and said he would bring over Mitía and her family—anything she wanted. But he was too old for her, and she liked her freedom. He reminded her of David, a rooster who wanted to rule his house.

Chava knew the only way to escape the suitor was to leave Doris and David's house. She met a divorced Englishwoman named Brenda and agreed to live in her apartment, sharing a room with her six-year-old son for two months. She then found lodging with una Americana and assisted her with household tasks.

My mom kept working at different factories depending on the hiring cycle. At one of these jobs, she learned a valuable lesson. Since her English was poor, the other women told my mom to say "Shut up" to the forewoman the next time she said something to her. She did as she was told while the other women watched and giggled. The forewoman, however, figured out the real story and told Chava: "Don't repeat what people tell you to say if you don't know what it means."

Also during this period, Lucy, a friend of Doris, told Chava she wanted to introduce her to a Mexican friend named Rosendo. Chava said no, influenced in part by Doris, who did not like Mexicans. My mom did date other men, but when they got serious, she told them she was returning to Colombia. She enjoyed her treachery, laughingly telling me it worked every time. My mom was almost thirty years old, but felt no need to settle down. Lucy was persistent over two years, and Chava finally agreed to accompany Rosendo to a wedding as a blind date.

This interview was a valiant attempt to ask questions despite our family mandate of silence. Nevertheless, I skipped over huge emotional moments because that is how we had always done things. I tracked my parents' emotional responses, and even though I was as traviesa as my mom, I still attempted to be a good daughter when possible. These unspoken sorrows cast gray clouds over our family. I didn't know it then, but the rain clouds had already been seeded for years in my father's most secret valley.

3.
Between Independence and Security

PEOPLE ARE OFTEN SURPRISED TO FIND MY LIFE springs from both México and Colombia. "What an interesting combination," they say, as if married people should always come from the same country. My parents *were* an odd couple from the beginning, but not because of their countries of origin.

Rosendo, the not-to-be trusted Mexican, called la Colombiana and arranged to pick her up for the wedding. She dressed like a doll, with precisely matching dress, high heels, and purse. He passed by her the first time, thinking: "Look at that loca all dressed up." He then realized it must be his blind date, and picked her up.

That first meeting highlighted their initial and ongoing differences. She had finished a year of college, worked at a bank, and been trained in her tía's upper-crust manners. He was más brusco, más tosco. Even the words sounded rough around the edges. In his own words, he was un indio chased down the mountain by drums.

They drove to the wedding and met up with his friend, Arturo, who, according to my mother, was a loco. She was the only non-Mexican at the wedding and felt both comfortable and awkward. While my mom could be very gregarious, in new settings she was often shy. He obliged with her request to be home by six p.m. Chava liked him, but she didn't let on, or at least she didn't think she did. My mom had learned how to read people to survive, and her intuition told her to keep the upper hand with this Mexicano.

My father saw her as a delicious conquest, this attractive, light-skinned Colombiana who did not appear to be captivated by him, like most of the women with whom he flirted. He called her regularly and they went out, often with Arturo. My dad had a definitive plan each time, and he saw she enjoyed their trips out of the city to Palm Springs or Borrego Springs. She rarely talked about her weekday grind at the factory, and enjoyed being the center of attention initially. My dad listened to her stories and methodically collected information for later use. He was amused to see she thought she was in control.

Eventually, as with her past novios who began to get serious, my mom decided to cool things down. She told him she was returning to Colombia soon. Satisfied with her plan of deceit, my mom was surprised to pick up the phone several weeks later and hear his playful voice. Maybe this was what she was waiting for: a man to call her bluff.

My dad was also good at reading people for the same reasons as my mom. He knew she was alone and that she wanted to stay in the US. She wore her heart on her sleeve, desperately covering it up with her chistes and criticism of his manners. Catching her en una mentira gave him power. She craved social acceptance as a newcomer, and she did not receive admiration in the 1950s for her erstwhile feminism.

So much of life is timing. My mom was tired of eating alone and working in factories where she was at the whim of bosses deciding who got work and for how long. She was weary of people smiling at her initially until they heard her thickly accented English. Their smiles faded, reminding my mom she was not one of them. This sense of isolation was compounded when her brother and sister talked about their marriages and growing families in Colombia, and she dodged their questions about her own prospects for marriage. She was torn between her independence and a sense of security.

My mom resumed going out with my dad the next weekend and the weekend after that, often double dating with Arturo and his güera girlfriend, Sharlene.

This was where the interview with my mom ended, and we never picked up that thread to see where her story unraveled. We never got to the piece of cloth worn thin by deceit and stitched together by loyalty.

The choice in front of my mom was to marry this indio from México and hope she didn't grow old and bitter, hope that his charm was only for her. She saw a sweetness in my dad despite the distance he placed between them when she probed into his past, asking why he had not married. He had never met the right woman he said, flashing his smile and daring her to push past the answer she wanted to believe. There was something unfinished in his life, like a small rain cloud that wrinkled his brow at times and made his tone terse.

My mom had not quite made up her mind about my dad when she discovered she was pregnant.

4.
Maldito Dreams

THE SECRET CHAVA SENSED WITHIN MY DAD'S silences was named Teresita del nino Jesús Durand. None of us knew how they met, although it could have been when he was a worker at one of her family's molinas. Teresita was the eldest of three children of the patriarch and matriarch of la familia Durand. My dad met her around 1945 when he was twenty-four. He may have thought she was his door out of the working class life he saw stretching out before him. He may have truly loved her. It is possible she went against her parents' wishes in choosing him.

Born Rosendo del Sagrado Corazón de Jesús Manrique González on April 17, 1921 in el Distrito Federal, my dad was raised by his mother, Concepción González Hernández. His father, Rosendo Manrique de Lara, had died five months before his birth from pneumonia. His mother worked in a restaurant, just scraping by. He was short and the color of caramel and his formal education stopped at the sixth grade. Like my mom, he was ambitious and smart and likely pushed himself to move into higher positions wherever he worked.

He was never going to attain his secret ambitions by marrying into a family of some wealth, but he tried, working in the family molinas. He learned how much he

wanted to be out from under Teresita's father and her middle brother Guillermo. He soon accepted he would not
be given the authority his brother-in-law exercised, even
though his efforts and intelligence were acknowledged.

Despite Teresita's resistance, he traveled to the US with
his friend Arturo, drawn by Arturo's stories of working in
big, fancy hotels and the women he met there. My dad was
bone tired every night in México and exhilarated when
Arturo and he threw suitcases into the back of his car for
the increasingly more frequent drives across the border.

I imagine my father, who was a good liar, inventing stories about his trips. The regalos he bought and distributed
to his growing family kept up the pretense that his forays
were not a serious threat to their lives.

Meanwhile, Teresita had borne my dad his second
child, a son we would meet twenty-five years later. My
dad then made a decision that tainted Teresita's and his
children's lives, and also created the opportunity for my
life. He was offered a job en el norte where he would earn
in two weeks what he earned in México in three months.
He already had a new passport, inventing an unmarried
businessman whose last name was González, and whose
motive for travel was to "radicar con familiares."

This initial step leading to my future existence was in
my possession for at least ten years before I read the fine
print, running my fingers across the written proof of his
engaño that concluded with his final journey north.

Had my dad really thought Teresita would join him,
as he told Miguel many years later? Did he think another
baby would tie her more to him than to her parents and
patria? Loving her father and obeying him was second
nature to Teresita . Loving her husband was easy early on,

but more difficult as he shut down. Working late when he was in town, my dad then went out regularly with Arturo, who was known as a playboy. If he had tried to tell Teresita that he wanted more than what México offered, she would not have listened, as she was not my mother, an orphan without the tightknit familia Teresita had. She feared he would leave her for his maldito dreams. Teresita would have known in her heart that she never had a chance to hold his reins in México.

His compadre Alfonso, brother of Arturo, had lived near Teresita's family in México and he was often the "telephone" of information back and forth between my father and his first familia, letting him know when his third child was born. My dad did not see this child until she was walking and talking.

Why did my father not begin fresh and end his relationship with Teresita ? Did he just want to have two, or even more, choices?

5.
The Road Is Forward

M Y FATHER'S SECOND FAMILY WAS OFFICIALLY entered in the records with Susan's birth on Mexican Independence Day, September 16, 1956. Their marriage four months later, in December, was the second piece of this puzzle. They hid this secret for many years, the problematic beginning to their courtship and marriage.

Perhaps it was then that Tot coined one of his favorite dicho: there are no problems, only situations. His job as a dishwasher at the Ambassador Hotel forced him to learn more about power and rules. Proper etiquette, showing up on time, working longer than paid for, and doing better than expected were his dictums. He watched the waiters until he could do it better. He had a good ear and listened to English television, practicing on the long drives to work until his accent disappeared. He was promoted to waiter.

The road is forward, I imagined him saying to himself as he drove away from his modest home, his hands grasping and ungrasping the wheel. He mastered the complex world of large hotel banquets: how to fold napkins into bishop's hats, fans, and pyramids and how to set tables with utensils placed in the order of use from the outside in, aligning each with the precision of a chess piece.

Mom would have encouraged his advancement with her advice: "Comb your hair back so it is straight. Do you have to play so much fútbol? Stay out of the sun or wear a big hat. Why don't you look for a job at a better hotel?"

❧

My mother traveled to Colombia alone with Susan, who was ten months old, to bring Gloria, who was thirteen, to the US in the summer of 1957. This was just before Susan's first birthday and soon after Mom realized she was pregnant with me. Gloria did not want to leave the only mother she knew, especially because her relationship with my mom was not that of beloved sisters. But now my mother wanted her to help with what would soon be two babies in diapers.

Mitía told my mom to bring her marriage certificate to Colombia so there would be no unpleasant questions. According to Gloria, my mother told her that was ridiculous, that people could think what they wanted. She knew the dates on the certificate would not quell people's whispered intimations.

Soon after they returned, Tot made his final trip to his Mexican familia, saying he was going to visit his mother. He arrived at Teresita's house in a Cadillac. Miguel, who was around five, remembers climbing in to touch the smooth leather and spin the steering wheel back and forth while Tot ventured inside the house. His parents talked a long time and anyone listening would have known they were disagreeing. He came back and lifted his son out, kissed and hugged him, and said goodbye. As he drove away, Miguel stood barefoot on the sidewalk, watching the car disappear with no idea it would be the last time he saw his father for many years.

During this visit, México City suffered a huge earthquake. There was no news of this event in the US, and when her husband finally called, my mom was furious at his silence. He thought she would be worried about his safety. He returned with a silk rebozo for my mom, who did not understand the value, even when he said: "It is so fine it can be slid through my wedding ring." The ring he had removed while in México.

By the time I was born six months after his last visit, Tot had cut his financial and emotional ties to Teresita and their children. My brother, whom we called Eddy, but whose birth name was Rosendo Eduardo, was born in 1961. My father cemented his life as Rosendo Amador González, a man married to Isabel Pinzón, with three children living in Glendale, California.

Mom confided in me years later that she had wanted her tubes tied after me, but Kaiser refused to perform the procedure until she had three children. Depressed about having another girl, she shed tears quietly in between changing diapers for two daughters. She often told the story of how one night I was crying, she was tearing her hair out, and my father came and took me from her. He started patting my back and walking me and saying, "Ay, pobrecita mija, her mom wants to throw her in the trash."

I never thought the story was funny and hid my sadness behind a forced smile. She also told me I was a colicky baby who could not be consoled. Babies are naturally moral beings who easily pick up cues from the environment. Once my brother was born, the doubt I carried in my heart about my importance was confirmed. Not only was he a boy, he was also the youngest, since my mom got her wish to be done with any further pregnancies.

❧

Economically, there was enough in the early years of their marriage to pay for the rent, the telephone, and food prepared at home. Throughout my early life, we bought most of our socks and basic household items at Sunday morning swap meets, attending the Holy Church of Frugality and Common Sense.

My mother was very organized, sitting at the kitchen table, adding up bills and figuring out her budget to cover costs for first six and then seven people when Mitía came to live with us in 1960.

Gloria recalls a particular trip to the beach, a favorite place for us to go on weekends to escape the inland heat. The car broke down and my parents had to borrow the twenty cents left of her small allowance to buy a loaf of bread. My mother parceled out the slices while we waited for Arturo to come and figure out what was wrong with the car.

❧

Mitía died only ten months after her arrival from complications of pneumonia, four months before Eddy turned one. With her death, Gloria, my mom's adopted sister, lost her mother, her connection to Colombia, and any remaining joy in her corazón. While Mitía had also raised my mom, she did not speak of Mitía in the loving way Gloria did, who called her "Mamá."

Despite her youth and resistance to coming, Gloria had been my family's salvation for five years. Not only because she was industrious in helping my mom with chores and childcare, but because Gloria was full of love and cariño in a home where my parents were more concerned with the tasks of feeding, clothing, and disciplining children than the comforting of tears. Gloria fed and bathed us por supuesto, but she also kissed us, whispered sweet nothings, and posed us for photos. In the one I love most, I am sitting on a tree stump with a big smile, my hands open wide to the world, inviting in joy.

But Gloria struggled under my father's strict rules and mistrusting gaze. He expected her home at three-thirty sharp. If she stopped to chat with a friend or to pick up a book from the library, he would turn up at the school in his car: "Why aren't you home? What were you doing?" She considered herself a "nerd" and never got into trouble, but it proved impossible to make him happy.

At the end of one semester, she brought home her report card, excited to show what she had accomplished: three A's and two B's. "Oh," he said coldly. "You could have gotten all A's."

Truly hurt, she thought, *It's not worth it. Nothing is good enough. No vale la pena matarse.*

She decided she had to flee his stern demeanor. This intensified as she stepped into her teens, and when Mitía died, Gloria's sadness did not escape my father's critical eye. Tot told her he would buy her a ticket to visit Colombia, so she could see that what she missed was long gone.

Just as she was preparing for her month-long trip, Tot felt a weakness begin in his feet and hands that spread within a week to his legs and arms, and his strength diminished. He had contracted a brain and nervous system disorder. We were too little to understand the exact diagnosis and we never discussed it when we were older. It may have been Guillain-Barré syndrome (GBS), a rare condition where the body's immune system attacks part of the nervous system.

Despite the anguish in her soul for Chava's difficulties, Gloria held fast with her plans and departed for Colombia, breathing freer as she flew far from my father's mandates. After five days, she sadly but firmly told my mother: "I'm not coming back." My mom asked her several times to come back, but she could not return to my father's harsh scrutiny.

My mom, at thirty-six, was alone with a sick husband and three children under the age of six. Every week she drove us an hour to the rehabilitation center in Santa Monica to visit Tot, who was in a wheelchair, too weak to even tear a napkin. I was scared, looking at him so feeble and quiet, not at all the man I feared at home, the man who only had to touch his belt buckle for us to obey him.

At home, Gloria's absence left a gaping hole of sweetness in my heart. She had been like the soft protective covers put on table corners, cushioning me from our parents' sharp edges so it didn't hurt as much if I bumped into their anger. I was four years old, and the days grew cold with my mother's worries and my father's slow, arduous recuperation. What I remember most after Gloria left is that we did not talk much, we did not sing much, and we rarely cried. Love, time, and even space felt scarce, even though three people were gone from the small house.

My mom kept prioritizing tasks to meet the minimal necessities of four people with very different needs. Anxiety about money mixed with the bitterness of losing Mitía and Gloria and the uncertainty of Tot's recovery.

After many months, Tot recovered fully and we brought him home. He was still frail and spent much of his first months resting on the couch. My mom bustled around him while changing Eddy's diapers, shushing us or sending us out to the backyard to play. It was then I formed an image of my mom as the stronger parent, the one who would not be slain by life's arrows.

For a few years it was just the five of us. My father eventually returned to work and the rhythm of the family settled. Neighborhood kids came to frolic in a four-foot tall plastic pool my father set up on the back patio. Outings to Disneyland, Descanso Gardens, and Venice Beach resumed, but the warm breeze of sweet love was gone; except for a moment here and there, when one or the other parent would rest a hand on our arm like the butterfly that lands on a flower and then is gone.

Susan entered Kindergarten unable to speak English. She brought home her fear, confusion, and *See Spot Run* books. This harsh language wooed me, especially on the small black and white TV. Books became my friends por vida. I readily accepted Susan's efforts to teach me to read, as I could tell this was going to help me avoid her sadness.

৵

We moved to our second home in La Crescenta. Tot brought his mother up from México to live with us. When my abuela moved in, there was no fond welcome from my mom. Abuela's high, tight voice battled my mother's more guttural shouts on an almost daily basis, and I spent more time outside to avoid their fights. They were two cats, the low and high growls, raised shoulders, and small, clawed paws waving near each other, both frustrated that my father didn't take sides. Really, he took the side that said women were petty y exageradas.

Abuela was understandably cranky and unhappy to be living in this strange land with a family who did not give her value or respect. She was a short woman with dark brown skin and straight gray hair she divided down the middle and let fall just above her shoulders.

The only time we ever made Mexican tamales was when she lived with us. She sat at the kitchen table, the cornhusks in a pile as she carefully pulled chicken from the bone, using the same bowl we used for salads, the same bowl that still resides in Susan's kitchen, full of thin cracks and many years of memories.

"Abuela, ven a comer," were the most common words she heard from her grandchildren.

Our new abode was a child's delight. Up on a hillside, it had three real bedrooms and stairs that led down to a large recreation and storage room. The downstairs door opened onto a lush lawn, a large covered patio to the right, and a beautiful crystal blue pool with a diving board.

My cousin, Maria Elisa, daughter of my mother's brother Luis, came to live with us for two years to study and learn English, increasing the household to seven again.

My father secured a higher paying job at the International Hotel near the Los Angeles airport, extending his drive from less than half an hour to almost an hour each way. Maria Elisa kept my mother company and helped with the chores. She stayed busy with school, learning English, and spending time with her best friend Idalid. My father was less demanding of her, his added work schedule causing him to leave the house and child oversight to my mom.

This setting was, on the surface, idyllic, with lots of playmates, the Southern California sun, and the only pool on the block. We often chased each other to the end of the cul-de-sac I called a "not through street" to play at Two Strike Park, crossing a bridge over a concrete water channel. Our world was still split in two, with Spanish inside our walls and English outside.

In the new home, when Susan entered second grade and I entered kindergarten at Monte Vista Elementary School, I was the only child who already knew how to read. My stay-at-home mom let her seven- and five-year-old daughters walk by themselves to school five blocks away. By itself, it may not have been significant, as crime was not a big issue in suburban La Crescenta. In many ways Mom set us all free very early, and we learned how to fall down, scrape our knees, get up, and find our own Band-Aids.

This was the house when I realized my mom's signing of Mamy on gifts was the same handwriting as Santa Claus. "Mamy" was one of her inimitable attempts to mix her two cultures, combining Mami with Mommy. I didn't feel disappointed or betrayed about her parental trick—I just wanted the presents.

My own daughter, with perhaps the same nonchalance, told me when she was nine: "It's kind of obvious there is no Santa Claus or tooth fairy. Trust me. I'm not falling for that anymore. I have evidence, like the handwriting." Damn. Unlike my mom, I had attempted to change my handwriting for a note I wrote from the tooth fairy. However, like my mom, I was not wedded to these caricatures, so I did not give it my all.

I wore my sister's hand-me-downs, hating that my mother always shopped at bargain stores and flea markets.

It's a struggle even now to see these events in the context of real poverty. Materially I had a lot—but my emotional, visceral response was that I never had enough.

❧

We made one final move to Mar Vista to decrease the work drive for my father. My parents bought their first and only house in a small suburb near Santa Monica. This occurred in an era when the construction of modest, inexpensive houses was on the upswing, as was the economy and the baby boomer era.

We again integrated into another white block, although no one followed suit in the thirty years my parents lived there. I was too young and sheltered in our silent integration process to notice the fights to uphold the Civil Rights Act. We found the other Latino families, one on each block around us, because we were all enrolled at St. Augustine, the closest Catholic school.

The house came with a tiny kitchen we squeezed into for eight years. Our parents then remodeled, adding a bigger kitchen and dining area in the back of the house and turning the old kitchen into a small den with the TV. I loved picking ripe plums, apricots, oranges, peaches, and avocados off our trees and the large lawn where we set up a badminton net.

❧

My abuela's daily presence and the memory of Tot's previous illness pushed Mom to find paid work. Once Eddy enrolled in kindergarten, she was always employed. While she would never have called herself a feminist, she sought her fulfillment beyond being a wife and mother through her work and art classes.

My mom's English improved and she intermixed both languages. It was a difficult practice for her, tortuous I am sure, given her ear was not wired to hear the subtle tones of languages or music. I still remember her practicing the words "eligible" and "illegible" for her business office work with patients at Kaiser, her pencil poised in her hand as she reviewed her notes.

"You are illegible for the operation. Your signature is eligible."

"No, Mom. Eligible for the operation, illegible signature." We would correct her and giggle at her struggles, arrogant and unsympathetic to her situation.

Within five years of our final move, Tot was promoted to banquet captain. He could congratulate himself that his sacrifices resulted into the life he imagined when he abandoned México. He and my mom were saving up with their two salaries to purchase another piece of property when the very first visitor from México came to the door.

6.
Odd and Out of Place

THE DOORBELL SIGNALED A VISITOR. MUFFEN yapped, running in tight circles and leaving a trickle of pee on the wood floor, impatiently looking for someone to open the door.

Having unearthed her papi's US home and firmly pressing the doorbell, Rosalinda stood still, eyes wide and expectant when he opened the door. His own eyes enlarged and he slammed the door shut, his hand squeezing the knob as his heart pounded and his breath quickened. On the other side of the door, Rosalinda stood, startled, waiting with her husband Juan José. Tot opened the door again and the look of susto was gone.

"I thought you were your mother."

He stepped aside and she came into his doble vida, one she had known about for many years. What goes through the head of a man whose past reaches out to bite him within the false lull of suburbia? He had turned his back on México and now he was caught too far away from shore to get to the beach, and not far enough out to dive under this wave.

We first met Rosalinda ever so briefly, like a wispy cloud that fades into the larger blue sky. Our home was more like the penumbra, that inbetweenness that families of different origins and languages move into without asking why. Arriving home from grammar school, we itched to get out of our uniforms and watch TV. Instead, Tot was sitting with a woman and man in the living room, which we knew, with sinking hearts, meant no TV. We said "hi" in our casual way and went toward our bedrooms, uninterested in yet more Spanish-speaking people.

"Is that how they greet you?" his first-born asked him.

What did it feel like to survey his youngest children from Rosalinda's perspective—did we seem appreciably better, worth his abandonment of his patria? Tot had gambled everything, going against his own inner integrity to recreate another family. He had to stand firm, assuring himself and these visitors this life was better.

They kept talking in Spanish, her voice full-throated and punctuated with laughter, my dad's voice the bass undertone, and her husband's voice a murmur. Muffen barked again, the signal that my mom was home. By now I was immersed in my Nancy Drew mystery that served as a giant earplug for my anxious brain. We didn't come out of our rooms, and he didn't ask us to. Storing this memory carefully and inaccurately, it floated among the horror of the My Lai Massacre and the Charles Manson murders that we were fed every night on the news.

Rosita, which I learned later is what Rosalinda was called by her familia, told me this story years later. My own memory only conjured up a fuzzy woman with no distinctive details at the front door. I thought the visit was brief, that she came alone, and I erased my mom from the scene altogether. Eddy's memory aligned with mine of a brief, abrupt door moment, but he was certain Mom was there. He remembered Rosita's gregariousness and Mom and Tot's discomfort with this clash of cultures and personalities. He felt it was a big deal, but there was a false nonchalance about it.

Susan's memory was more expansive. She would have been around thirteen, to my eleven and Eddy's eight. She vividly remembered us already in our bedrooms when someone came to the door. She heard two people speaking Spanish in the living room but couldn't recall who the other person was. She might have peeked through the bedroom door to see who was there, but timidity precluded her stepping out of her cocoon. It was more about hearing unknown voices.

Rosita did not stake a claim to join our familia. For her, the visit was significant; but unlike Miguel, she did not want to migrate. She had established herself with her husband and would soon begin her family. Eddy believed from the beginning that she was our sister, even though he didn't feel it.

Nobody said anything about Rosita after the visit, even when we met Miguel five years later. You'd think someone would say: "Didn't someone else come to our house saying they were related to us?"

My abuela lived with us then and knew the detallitos of the entire story, but she kept silent. A year after Rosita's visit, she died, sealing lips that had acrid answers about my father's secrets.

Years later, Susan and I remained ambiguous about who Rosita was. The possibility lurked that she was our sister, but we did nothing to confirm it either way. There was no context for a woman to say she was our older sister—it was just too odd and out of place with our lives.

Susan's first real information about Rosalinda came from Mom. After Miguel's visit, Mom told Susan that

Rosalinda thought she was Tot's daughter but she wasn't. Her name was so similar to mine; why would a man give two daughters almost the same name? Susan thought there was a time after we met Miguel that Rosita came over to the house again, but her memory is blurred, like a photo taken without enough light. By that time, I was gone, using college as my escape hatch to find spaces where questions and answers were allowed.

❧

"Why didn't you come out?" Rosita asked Susan and me thirty years later in Acapulco.

Why indeed. We would have had to confront the lie underneath our family's existence and we were just children trying to fit in.

It was not until I was in my late thirties that my eldest sister emerged from the dust of our memories. We just kept hitting the delete button near our pinky fingers and carried on like our father and mother, celebrating birthdays and graduations and holidays as if the family bubble of five would never burst no matter how many people rang the doorbell.

Eddy saw Rosita a couple of times, once during a trip to Tijuana with her and my parents. He described her as wafting in strong perfume and using extravagant gestures, the way an introvert categorizes an extrovert. She was now a businesswoman, coming to Los Angeles regularly to buy clothes in the garment district and sell them in México. Eddy didn't tell me this right away, even though we were in regular contact.

Susan invited Rosalinda and Tot to her house for dinner a few times. She didn't invite Mom, knowing she couldn't deal with both a brother and sister from another woman. Rosalinda was "Papi this" and "Papi that" and Susan sat there watching, surprised Rosita didn't show any anger toward him. Rosalinda was very affectionate. Our parents rarely kissed or embraced each other and we were cautious expressing our cariño. Tot remained cold to Rosita's affection, he didn't become a different person simply because she was demonstrative.

Again, as with Eddy, no word to me until years later, as if we could keep this major life change insignificant by not talking about it. We squelched any possibility of shifting from the doble vida that Tot, and then Mom, assiduously and stubbornly protected. They were our parents, and we were not going to challenge them for people we neither knew nor understood.

Part 2:
Death

Me with my 6-month old twins;
Gina on left, Teo on right, 1996

Christmas with Miguel, 1977

7.
Shattered to Pieces

HOW ARE THINGS GOING DOWN THERE?" I ASKED Susan in a phone call a few weeks after the Northridge earthquake in 1994.

"Okay. There don't seem to be any more aftershocks," she replied.

I had been living in Berkeley for six years, and after experiencing the Loma Prieta earthquake, could easily recall how the shock of having the ground shake below my feet unsettled me for weeks.

There was another reason I had become unsettled after that quake five years earlier. Carolyn and I had met on a soccer field a month before. She was competitive like me and we had gone out a few times with friends after practice to have a beer. I had run into her in a downtown Oakland parking garage because we both worked for the county, she as a Public Defender and me as Child Protective Services supervisor. We were flirting on the phone in our respective Alameda County cubicles, making plans to watch the third game of the Bay Area World Series, when the buildings swayed from side to side. I ended up spending the night with her, and she became my first and only female lover.

A year later, at Thanksgiving, I did my own casual rendition of *Guess Who's Coming to Dinner*. "Hi, Mom. I'm bringing a friend down for Thanksgiving. Her name is Carolyn, she's on my soccer team."

"Oh, okay. Will you be staying here?"

"No, we'll stay at Susan and Fred's."

"Why isn't she with her family?"

"Her family is back east. We'll come over early to help."

When I developed a crush on another woman six months before meeting Carolyn, I veered off the heterosexual highway, thinking this was the identity unease that haunted me. The solidarity another woman provided attracted me in a world where I often felt invisible.

Carolyn seemed daring to me in her athletic pursuits and I followed her lead. We bought kayaks, and I came to know birds by their yellow feet or the white stripe that unfolded when they flew low across the seashore. I bought a high-quality bike at Carolyn's urging, although I never loved the hills as she did.

In a trip to the Maasai Mara in Kenya to visit two of her college friends, I learned hyenas were a matriarchal society and that lions often scavenged from them. Carolyn exposed me to the beauty of nature; and I lost the fear and discomfort I had learned from my parents, who thought nature was to be taken in measured doses.

We became season ticket holders to the Stanford Women's basketball team. I had had a challenging relationship with my alma mater, but I enjoyed reconnecting this way as an alumna.

Moving into her house in the Berkeley flatlands a year and a half after meeting, I ignored the yellow flags that had led to our several breakups. I told my parents I was moving in with her casually, letting them presume we were housemates. In my early thirties, this stab at establishing roots was glue for my nomadic soul, which had accumulated fifteen addresses since the time I scampered away from Mar Vista. I had always believed in couples having separate rooms, even if we mostly slept in the same bed at night.

My first live-in boyfriend and I had done so, too, and this set-up allowed me to keep my little secret for years. When my parents visited, I gave them my room and slept in the back room, which I used as my fledgling self-employment office.

After a few years together, we discussed becoming parents, something I would have passed on because of my experience with my mom. I was not convinced I wanted children, especially as I recovered from a series of negative job experiences, but Carolyn really wanted children and I felt selfish saying no. I also knew it meant telling my parents that Carolyn and I were not just housemates.

ઝ

"Do you have earthquake supplies?" I asked Susan.

"No, other than that Fred always buys enough food for a huge party every weekend!"

Susan had worked for Mexicana Airlines for a number of years before becoming a bilingual teacher. She had mentioned once that on a trip to México she had visited with Rosita, although she retained doubts about whether she was our sister. She had also met another woman, Tere, who Rosita had introduced her to on her most recent trip.

"So last week, I was watching the news with Tot and in a moment of not being my usual careful self, I asked him if Rosalinda was our sister. Do you know what he said? 'Yes.' I got bold and asked: What about Teresita? 'Yes.' ¿Lo puedes creer? Just like that."

It's not easy to shut up me up, but I flopped down on my bed like a rag doll, my eyes wide, my smile painted on. Three kids. They were older than us. We were Tot's second family. The news felt like a glacier toppling into the icy sea of my gut.

"This wasn't some no-big-deal relationship like we believed," I replied. "Was he married to their mom?"

I didn't want to hear the answer. My relationship to Tot was finally comfortable. He had melted some of his cold demeanor after retiring from the Century Plaza hotel.

"Miguel says so," said Susan.

"That means," I slowed down, "he married Mom when he was already married?"

"Guess so."

The silence sat between us as we surveyed the damage to the family portrait. I was still stuck on wanting a good relationship with Tot after all these years, a father who loved Don Quixote and had some of his flaws. Both believed in what they wanted to see rather than what was, and it was time to evaluate my father's motives and actions. I wanted a hero despite mounting evidence that Tot was merely mortal, as so many men are in the realm of women and deception.

"I need to get ready," Susan said. "We're going to Mom's for dinner. How are you doing?" Her voice switched tone and topic, as only she could. Drop a bomb and then go take a shower.

I followed her diversion because I was no more ready than she to ask difficult questions or feel the disappointment as the ice of denial melted. "Good," I said. "It's funny to think how worried I am about telling Mom and Tot about the possibility of them being grandparents again, when their story isn't Ozzie and Harriet either."

I hung up and rinsed plates, spoons, and wine glasses until the sink was empty and the dishwasher was almost full. There were no cleaning products stored under the sink to clean my head full of grime.

That day, when the truth came crashing down, there was nothing left to do but salvage something from these secrets. But I couldn't do it, couldn't slice away the story my birth was built around, and lay bare my dad's actions that led to my birth. I could say that I was immersed in my own journey to have kids, but I am not willing to be so kind. I did not have the wherewithal to accept the real story yet, so I tilted at the windmills in my life in a vain effort to hold off confronting the unpleasant truth.

I thought about how Tot had supported me through an incredibly difficult work situation just two years earlier. I had been fired for insubordination for standing up to my supervisor's harassment. Devastated, I had called him.

"Fight back—the rules will protect you."

He was preaching truth and fairness, and I believed him. Despite earlier work experiences where I had been suspended and demoted, I did not want to accept that power trumped truth, even though I had confirmation of Tot's doble vida for many years.

This double image of Tot, where he is urging me to fight back with truth against injustice while keeping his own culpability to himself, is what Susan had felt when meeting Miguel. I was very late getting on her train of doubt and fear. Meanwhile, our brothers had had conversations between themselves years before Susan and I spoke.

"Eddy invited me to eat at Tito's Tacos, saying they were very famous," said Miguel. "That's probably when we talked about my sisters, and which reminded me of Susan and of you."

Eddy only acknowledged that he knew early on we had two sisters when I asked him thirty years later. Even with Eddy, I didn't ask the questions that piled up in my head. *Why didn't you say something to us? What did you think about Tot having two families?*

I was pretty direct, but regarding Tot's doble vida I was, and had always been, as silent as my siblings. Susan, of all people, had dared to ask him a taboo question and he just answered it, como si nada. Some of my reticence was a tit for tat: you keep your familial secrets, and I'll keep my "alternative" lifestyle.

Tot and Mom were amazingly low-key about me being with a woman. They had not acknowledged the letter I'd sent a year earlier telling them that I was a lesbian and that we were planning to have a child.

In fact, after a complicated two years of visits to fertility experts, my partner was pregnant with twins, and I was the egg donor. We went to LA for a visit when Carolyn was about seven months pregnant, to give them a clear visual that their middle child was once again choosing the path less traveled. They smiled and were gracious, but no questions asked. I saw myself as being in the same boat as Miguel—not exactly the child you bring up in conversation with your friends.

੩੦

With the birth of my twins Gina and Teo in 1995, I had a taste of how far sacrifice and love can go. My loss of innocence around Tot's first family made me take a tentative, albeit bold step into my own new role as Mami. Like little children fascinated by their parents' shoes, I had stuck my feet into motherhood and was clomping around my familias and neighborhoods, feeling big and awkward at the same time.

Carolyn and I had created children without ever talking about making a lifelong commitment to each other. The closest we got was designing rings, but we never had any kind of ceremony, private or public. My guess is that we skipped some keys steps because they would have exposed the weakness in the foundation of our relationship. Instead, we redesigned the interior of her house, re-landscaped the yard, and became parents. Apart from our internal challenges, every act outside our inner circle meant constant explanation and exposure. Traveling with twins was like driving a special edition Harley Davidson motorcycle painted bright red.

"Twins. How cute. How was it carrying them? Was labor hard?"

"They were actually about the size of one big baby. We had a C-section."

"Do twins run in your family?"

"No, not really."

I didn't mean to lie, to keep our process a secret, but sometimes I just wanted to go shopping at Berkeley Bowl or take a walk around San Pablo Park—not explain my sexuality and our fertility process. Mostly I wanted to take a very long nap.

All through my twenties and thirties, English ruled my conversations with my parents with a sprinkling of Spanish words like carne and sábanas. Once my kids were born,

I shifted to Spanish, knowing they would get even more English exposure than I did. I translated all their books into Spanish, bought Spanish-language children's music, and asked my mom to speak to them in Spanish.

The problem was that my mom took her language cue from whoever spoke to her. If she heard English, she would respond in kind; if Spanish, she would respond in Spanish. I tested my hypothesis, switching languages back and forth and watching her, like Pavlov's dog, responding to my stimulus. Speaking Spanish to my children and my mom felt weird at first, like stumbling into a landscape full of recognizable yet treacherous terrain. The twins' birth had brought back the language of our niñez. Everyone in my immediate family spoke English now but had been reared in Spanish. My children took this legacy to another level, switching a pattern that had held for over thirty years.

I was determined to plant a new love pattern, too. Shaking off the dust from words of affection, I used them until they were no longer foreign to my tongue. Mi querido, mi vida, mi amor, mi cielo. These words never came from my mother's mouth. From her, I was more likely to hear "¡Cochina!" when I left my room messy, "¡Terca!" when I would stubbornly resist her advice, and the lovely and popular "¡Burra!" for no particular reason. My father had nicknames full of cariño for us, even if his demeanor was stern and his physical affectionate sparse. Susan was "Chupis," Eddy answered to "Papoon," and his apodo for me was "Muñeca."

I looked forward to seeing my parents now, appreciating their willingness to be abuelos even if the circumstances were not part of their rulebook. We went out dancing to celebrate my thirty-eighth birthday on a visit to Los Angeles, leaving my six-month old twins with their abuelos. When we stepped back inside their house at midnight, my mom was sitting in the den with Teo, who smiled at us as if he always hung out with his abuela at this hour.

"¿Y Gina?" I whispered.

"Con tu papá in our room."

I walked to their bedroom and peeked in. There he was, half-awake with Gina snoozing next to him. I was embarrassed that my kids had kept their abuelos up late and equally pleased at such sweet pictures of cariño.

"She's kind of stiff." He sat up and gazed at mi hija.

"Yeah, her body can do that in a new situation." I leaned in and carefully cradled her in my arms.

"Good night, Tot. Thanks."

Even if they weren't the most cuddly parents or abuelos, they could take care of business. Except for this second family business.

ã€š

When my family of four drove to LA for my nephew Rafael's graduation from eighth grade in June, I convinced everyone in my LA family to go to The Golden Pagoda in downtown Chinatown, where we always went as kids. It was still beautiful to me with yellow, red, and blue trim on the outside and lush red colors inside. As Susan and I walked together into the restaurant, we silently noticed how difficult it was for Tot to climb the stairs, his breathing becoming short and his right leg swollen. Even though his physical condition slowly worsened, we did not ask questions about what was wrong. Fred, Susan's husband, simply gave him an arm tonight while the rest of us waited patiently.

That was just the beginning of our night, then, and as kids. We were lured after dinner by the sound of the organ grinder with a small monkey who rejected pennies from our hands; he only wanted silver coins. That tiny face, then and now, evoked smiles, with little thought to his life beyond the plaza. We closed out the evening at the wishing pond, where we used to beg our parents for pennies to throw, the wishes not as important as the toss, splash, drop of the coin to the bottom.

Tonight, we watched as Rafael and Steven hoisted Gina and Teo up to throw their first pennies. They did not yet know what wishes were and how they could sidetrack your life.

8.
Día de los Muertos

TOT TRIED TO TELL ME HE WAS DYING. I WAS SITting in his TV room, an awkwardly shaped space at the front of their home, originally the kitchen when Rosita first stepped in the house. We had come down for Susan's fortieth birthday. The kids were napping and I rested in his dark brown recliner, loving the feel of the soft, velour-like cloth on my bare legs and arms. He came in with a manila envelope in his hand.

"Hi, beautiful." He had begun saludandome así in the last five years or so.

"I can get up, Tot."

I started to move, but he put his hand out.

"No te preocupes; this won't take long."

He sat down on a low stool, catching his breath, the quiet rasp now a common sound.

"Here."

He pulled a stack of papers out of the envelope.

"This is my durable power of attorney and a copy of your mom's and my trust. I put you down as the first person to make decisions if I am sick. You're tough. Susan won't be able to make the hard decisions."

I looked at him and didn't comprehend his words; they refused to penetrate the wax that coated my denial. Taking my cue from him, as I always had, I held out my hands for the papers, keeping my question about hard decisions in a far-away bottom drawer.

"Okay."

He got up and ambled out. The shuffle of his pantuflas faded as he neared the kitchen, the chair legs scraping the cream-colored tiles, his Spanish mixing in with my mother's. I remember hearing the same sounds while I lay in my childhood bed, the rise and fall of their voices drifting down the hall. I fell asleep, the manila envelope falling to the floor.

As we said goodbye the next day, he slipped me a fifty-dollar bill. "Para tus chuchulucos."

This was a generous, loving gesture he often made now as we said goodbye. I never asked what chuchulucos meant, intuitively knowing it was for whatever I needed or wanted.

The next time I spoke to Tot was on a Tuesday a month and a half later. He asked about the children since Halloween was in two days and remarked that my mom was out buying dulces for the trick-or-treaters.

"I was too tired to go with—" his coughing cut off our conversation.

I waited, holding my breath and gripping the phone as one hacking cough flowed into another into another, like waves crashing on a rocky shore, tearing at my ears, filling my head with gravelly sand. The phone clicked and the dial tone droned.

Scared to call him, I waited a few moments for him to call me, for him to make it all right again. When he didn't, I picked up *Moo, Baa, La La La!* and handed the book to Gina as I scanned the mottled sky for signs of the predicted rain. The Berkeley flatlands did not give enough of a view to tell whether darker clouds followed the grey tinged ones.

Moving the African violet and the delicately painted clay pot from New Mexico, I crowded them onto the left side of the mantel. As I laid out the embroidered cloth from Colombia and prepared my altar for Día de los Muertos, I sank into the truth—my father was dying, his lungs losing the battle for oxygen. He would not live to see my twins celebrate another birthday. I smoothed the beige cotton fabric with shaking hands and rubbed the tiny cross-stitched flowers along the border. I placed two velas on the cloth, yearning to light them so they could burn away my terror. I squeezed my pain down into the pit of my stomach and promised myself to call him after dinner, willing myself to get back on task.

It was my first altar, spurred by a visit I'd made with my parents the year before to the Oakland Museum's annual exhibit. The idea of honoring my antepasados struck a chord in me that my parents had never nurtured; this was a tradition Tot didn't speak of or practice. Even though we were figuring out costumes for the twins' first official Halloween, I did not enjoy the negative portrayal of witches and cats or the gross amounts of candy scooped up by little kids.

After dinner and the children's bedtime routine of a book and song for each, I sat quietly in the living room, unable to voice my fears about Tot to Carolyn or to call my siblings. The reality of creating an altar with the very real possibility that my father's picture would be on my altar next year ripped at the seams of my heart.

I waited until Carolyn turned off the bedroom light to blow my nose, tiptoe in, and pull the covers up around my ears.

Susan phoned the next night around ten to say Tot couldn't breathe, even with the oxygen tank, and had been taken to the hospital in an ambulance.

"Should I come down?" I asked her.

"No. Wait until tomorrow to see how things go."

I hung up and fear twisted through my body as I lay in bed, remembering my premonition but not giving it enough space to guide me. When Teo's cries woke me two hours later, I stepped into my worn pantuflas and scuffled toward his room, stroking his shaking back and singing "Duermase mi niño, duermase mi rey" until his breathing relaxed. He and Gina had turned one in August, and he still didn't sleep through the night.

Friday morning Susan said Tot would stay over the weekend for "observation." Eddy and I booked flights for the evening, leaving out of Oakland. As I packed, a persistent voice whispered, "Vete, niña, vete, get on the plane now."

I placed a picture of my abuela making tamales on the altar. Hers was the only death I had experienced, a difficult grief as our relationship was not warm. I'd shop for marigolds and papel picado when I returned on Monday. The altar would have to be bare bones for now.

At eleven a.m. I got the final call from Susan. "Linda." Her voice was too high. "Tot's dying. You have to come."

"Oh, God. Can I talk to him?"

"Okay, but make it short," she admonished me.

The sound of his wheezing, as if someone was choking him, dissolved my heart, turning my denial into a hot, wet mess. I sobbed, my breath short and choppy.

"Te quiero, Tot, te quiero. Don't die," I begged.

Susan's voice interrupted me. "You have to calm down. You're agitating him."

"Okay, Okay. I'm calm." I sucked in my tears and listened to the sound of him futilely gulping at air. "I'm coming to see you, Tot. Te quiero."

I made myself hang up and leave him, blew my nose and began dialing other numbers. Yes, there was room on the twelve-thirty p.m. Oakland flight. Yes, Carolyn could meet me at childcare. Yes, Eddy would try to make it from Pacifica. Mientras tanto, trying to figure out what to bring for a funeral I did not want to ever take place.

Half an hour later, Carolyn and I hoisted our two squirming chiquitos into their car seats, and I steadied my hands enough to buckle the five-point seatbelts. I drove the endless fifteen minutes to the airport, pushing my panic into the asphalt through the gas pedal. The kids' chatter forced me to keep pulling my heavy foot off the gas again and again.

Carolyn helped me haul car seats, umbrella strollers, and suitcases into the curbside check-in line and drove off to find parking. Eddy and his wife, Shan-Yee, arrived a few minutes later and grabbed the car seats and we passed through security and onto the plane. We collapsed into the first set of facing seats and busied ourselves acomodando a los niños.

Carolyn scooted in as the flight attendant was closing the door, her face flushed red from parking the car and running to make the flight. I sighed with relief.

While Shan-Yee and Carolyn entertained the kids, Eddy and I sat with unspoken words between us. His lizard-like stillness was in contrast to my hands, clenching and unclenching on my lap, urging the plane forward con toda prisa. We arrived an interminable hour later at LAX, where I found the nearest bank of telephones. When they transferred me to another room, I knew.

"He's with the ángeles, hija," Mom said, her voice crumpled with grief.

I leaned against the thin metal divider between phones, shook my head at my brother, squeezed my lips together.

Day of the Dead. I wanted to find a little corner here, maybe in the phone bank, and leave a recuerdo, like the white crosses placed on the highways in México where someone had died, with flowers and fotos and my tear stains. Instead, I walked silently with my troupe toward the exit doors. When we entered the hospital room, I recoiled when kissing Tot on the cheek, the cold skin like a glass of water flung in my face, wiping away any disavowal that his body had finished its work on this earth.

෴

Two days later, I gazed up at the peaked roof of St. Augustine church, gray and foreboding across from MGM Studios. The limousine carrying my family turned left into the parking lot. My pockets stocked with tissues, I sat tense and motionless in the back seat with my mother, Susan, and my two brothers. My father's two other daughters were in México, and I didn't think of them at all. I learned later that Miguel had called them.

To my left, a two-story stucco building with Spanish tiles on the roof housed the grammar school I had attended for seven years. I reached over and patted my mom's hand; she gripped mine with unexpected ferocity. We never held hands. It took the death of her esposo of forty years to give me what I had yearned for, yet without knowing it until our palms touched. We were not of the breed of Latin American *mujeres* strolling down the *mercado* or through the *plaza*, arm in arm, leaning in to exchange *chisme* about neighbors.

My veins were not yet as pronounced as hers, but the pattern of wrinkles, the slender yet sturdy fingers matched up perfectly. Her eyes stared straight ahead, her lips pursing and unpursing. She had not done much to her hair, the short waves more askew than usual, a small line of gray visible above her forehead. As the car stopped, her grip tightened. The nails pressed painfully into my skin. I pulled my hand away from her pain when we slid out of the limo, wanting to receive comfort rather than give it. As I trailed my mom, the certainty of death slipped into my soul.

The Pérez clan arrived at the same time, spilling out of a Pontiac Firebird and a Dodge station wagon. Led by Carlos, the mustached patriarch who coached my sister Susan and I in our fledgling soccer days, they surrounded us, their warm-heartedness palpable. I embraced Laura, now a *señora* with her three children in tow. Her sweet voice soothed me. I glimpsed the oldest son, Lorenzo, as he locked the Firebird, noticing his prominent cheekbones and lips, recalling the thrill and shame of making out with him years past in the back seat of a car. Falling into the ample arms of the matriarch, Rosa, I searched her round face full of *cariño* and found a smile promising me that I would one day feel joy again.

Rosa then turned to hug my mother, petite and stiff, with her sharp angled face and drooping lips. "Lo siento mucho, Isabel."

My mother pulled away abruptly, and I left her despair to enter the back of the church. The austere organ music wafted down from the choir loft to those gathering to view the body of the man we knew as Rosendo Amador González, dead at seventy-five. The open casket stared at me in the dark vestibule, daring me to approach. My dad was unbreakable for me. Even as secret after secret had shredded my innocence, he stuck to his position; and I wanted that zone of certainty.

A swift left to the women's bathroom gave me time to hide the tears. I was glad I did not wear mascara, for it would have been smeared like Susan's, who pushed open the wooden door as I turned to leave. I stayed back and handed her a tissue.

We squeezed hands briefly and entered the vestibule, filling with people. Susan greeted people easily. Filled with anxiety, I darted straight through to enter the church proper, avoiding speaking my first language. That Spanish was my first language was a secret even to me for many years.

❧

In my late twenties, I had worked as an MSW intern in an East Los Angeles mental health clinic. Providing therapy in Spanish had challenged my lazy lengua and my facile assertion of being bilingual on my job applications.

In a supervisory session halfway through my internship, a psychologist asked me: "What is your first language?"

I paused. "Spanish."

It slid out like ivy through a fence, determined to cross the border. I knew it was true, but it felt hollow. So much had been lost since I was a toddler, and I didn't yet know the way back.

Español was a better friend now, one I included on important trips and invited to our birthday parties, even dreamt in on occasion. Español y yo tussled over complex words, but we forgave each other con un besito.

Walking to the glass-enclosed family room near the front of the church, I made a half-genuflecting motion at the front pew before turning right. Carolyn was arranging the twins' snacks, toys, and blankets with the help of Maria Elena, my sister's childhood friend. Seeing her whisper with Carolyn lessened the pounding in my head.

I corralled Teo, who was running around the five sets of pews like a newly caged animal, his round face and mischievous hazel eyes looking into my dark ones for comfort in these strange surroundings. Since he and Gina began walking three months earlier near their first birthday, our adventures had risen to new heights, including the end tables and bathroom counter. I was grateful for their bountiful energy and how they turned this room full of hard wooden benches into a playground.

"¿Quieres algo de tomar?" I asked him.

Teo nodded, and I carried him to his blue backpack to find a sippie cup. My left eye twitched. I pressed my finger gently into the hollow below my eyebrow. I handed Teo to Maria Elena, knowing Gina was less comfortable with strangers and would snuggle up to Carolyn after she had run off her energy. I gave mi querida hija's dark head a besito and ran my hand across the cheek of her small heart-shaped face.

As I left the family room, an ancient ache radiated through my blood, a silent echo that bounced off the stained glass windows full of saints. I used to know them by name until I graduated from high school. My parents' allergy to organized religion had not daunted me. I did not like the nuns who could hit us for my first few years in a Catholic school, but I found comfort in the rituals and incense.

I broke up with Jesus in my mid-twenties, when I needed help on a trip to New York and he did not answer the way I wanted. Wandering in a spiritual desert for over ten years, I had dabbled in mantras, therapy, and self-help workshops with no purpose other than mobilizing enough energy to get through another day. Today I wished my efforts had been more fruitful so I could make sense of Tot's life and death.

Susan's eldest son, Rafael, stood forlornly just inside the big paneled doors of the main sanctuary. His love ran deep for his abuelo, and I hugged him, his husky adolescent body already dwarfing mine. As he leaned into me, I planted my feet and let his sobs fill our lonely corner.

If my parents had been any good with American idioms, one they would have used was: "Crying is for the weak." Or better yet: "No use crying," not even at a funeral.

Mary stood regally on a pedestal, her alabaster palms opened toward us above the glow of the velitas that cast flickering shadows on our silhouette. This Mary did not resemble the María we picked for the prayer cards. Ours was full of vibrant reds, greens and golds; her skin tone darker, the angel below her with brown hair. I had not developed that sweet relationship many Mexicanos have with La Virgen de Guadalupe.

As Rafael and I walked down to the front pew, I saw several rows full of Mexicans in the church—mostly waiters from my father's years as a banquet captain. They were at his funeral today, but they had never come to our home.

He kept them for himself, and I wondered what special role they played for him that he had excluded from us, what knowledge they had of his life that he did not want to slip out.

꙳

The last time I had occupied this front pew was three years earlier, when Tot surprised Mom with a service to renew their wedding vows on her birthday. A few phone calls to their three grown children and an awkward visit with the priest paved the way. I squirmed as my dad answered the priest's question about how many children he had with "three." Still, I did not correct my father in front of the priest.

Tot's plan was incongruous given his and my mom's lack of bond with the church and God. I doubt they set foot in a church once we were in high school, except for the occasional wedding, baptism or funeral. That was essentially true for all of us. Their spiritual anchor had been the sweat of their brows.

Susan and I told Mom that day to dress up for a birthday meal and then drove her into this parking lot.

"What are we doing here?"

"Just come, Mom."

We walked her through the side door and into the front of the church. My father was already there with Eddy and the priest.

"Oh, no. What is this?"

She was unexpectedly shy and abashed. It was a vulnerability I rarely glimpsed in my mom, wishing she had felt safe enough to share it with us more often. I nudged her forward and she looked at Tot, who was grinning at her.

"Ven, vieja," he said.

"Oh, Rosendo. ¿Que haces?"

She climbed the steps to stand with him, and the priest introduced himself.

I imagine now it was when he was beginning to feel ill, beginning to have silent conversations with death about what he should pack to take with him, what he was leaving behind. Tot was not driven by false optimism. In that we were alike: staunch realists with a touch of romance laced around our sharp edges. With that as a frame, I think it was his way of making amends, the church wedding they never had. His emotions were less hidden now that he saw the finish line to his life, the sadness and joy making his voice that much more dulce.

And my mom—did she have flashbacks to when they first met, to when she found out she was pregnant with Susan?

Their wedding had always been a gap, like a blank album page with shadows where something had been removed. No pictures, no stories, no wedding anniversary, just a vague recollection it had happened in December. They had wedding rings, they said they were married, and they lived like they were married. I had wondered sometimes if they married because my mom was already pregnant, as was the case for so many couples, and just moved the date back a few months.

When I researched county records, sitting in the Mormon temple's Family Search library many years later, I found nothing under 1955. I clicked forward and found them: December 26, 1956. The day after Christmas, three months after Susan's birth. Finding out that the marriage date was off by a year, a piece of data that had seemed definite, called every single piece of information into question.

Had my mom really not known about Tot's past and the two daughters that were not at the funeral?

I rose at my appointed time, walked up the three marble stairs and turned to the right of the elaborate altar, so different from the one I was creating in Berkeley. At the wooden podium, I read Ecclesiastes 3:1–8,

> "For everything there is a season,
> and a time for every matter under heaven . . .
> a time to love, and a time to hate;
> a time for war, and a time for peace."

As I strode back to the front pew, I fingered my silver and turquoise necklace, one of only three gifts Tot himself had bought me. The organ notes rose to the concrete arches crossed like spider webs above us.

Miguel and Gloria brought the bread and wine up to the priest and altar boys. While each of their entries into our home had been fraught by difficult relationships with Tot, over the years we had all relaxed more, and they were two people I'd counted on for laughter, dancing, and a good, strong hug and kiss when they came to visit. They were both family and not family—Miguel for being my half-brother, Gloria for being my tía without being related by blood. They were an unlikely pair. Miguel, with a now broad, ruddy face and extra weight that had settled slowly on his waistline over the twenty years since we met, was turned out in a dark blue suit and shiny, pointed shoes, his wavy hair slicked back. His usual grin was missing, the one that reminded me of Tot. Gloria was diminutive in comparison, dressed in her signature straight-line skirt and closed, comfortable pumps, her light brown hair carefully coiffed and her manner as serious as Miguel's.

Gloria had come back to Los Angeles in 1986 with her husband, Enrique, and their two children many years after she had fled my father's iron grip. As a grown woman who was not under Tot's thumb, she had graciously disagreed over the years when my father behaved poorly toward her. Tot *and* Mom drew Miguel and Gloria in and left them out cuando les daba la gana, and we had accepted this in some odd attempt to hang on to a semblance of normality. I acted out my unconscious childhood anger at Gloria for having left me as a little girl by silently agreeing to my parents' refusal to give her the place she deserved in our lives as our tía.

Gloria knew nothing about Tot's first family. She only remembered him mentioning an aunt who worked in Mexican films, who was maybe the sister of my abuela. Miguel was introduced casually to her as "Rosendo's son," and Gloria never asked my mom for details, out of respect. She joined the dance of silence while once again infusing our home with her cariño when she visited, undaunted by the atmosphere that still chilled my parents' home. I was twenty-eight by then and perceived my father's quiet comments about her effusiveness as a signal to me, the extrovert, to pipe down.

According to Gloria, when Tot was just visiting, he could be very pleasant. Despite their difficulties when she was young, once she returned, they struck up a cautious camaraderie. She remembers a trip to Tijuana with Enrique and my parents. They had stopped at a gas station before crossing the border and the women took turns holding the bathroom door open so they just paid once.

Gloria had asked Enrique several times if he wanted to use the bathroom and he kept saying no. Rosendo finally said: "Stop asking him. He doesn't want to pee in the United States, he wants to mear en México." That was how funny and sharp he could be when he wanted. If you did what he preferred, he would bend over backwards.

Eddy came up to the podium to read from the New Testament, 1 Corinthians 13:4–7. I was again struck by how much he looked like Billy Crystal, although Eddy's eyes and lips were larger and fuller. He shared Crystal's dry humor, tinged with sarcasm. His words were subdued and firm.

> "Love is patient, love is kind.
> It does not envy.
> Love is never boastful, nor conceited, nor rude;
> It is not self-seeking, nor easily angered.
> It keeps no record of wrongdoing.
> It does not delight in evil,
> But rejoices in the truth.
> It always protects, trusts, hopes, and preserves.
> There is nothing love cannot face;
> There is no limit to its faith, hope, and endurance.
> In a word, there are three things that last forever:
> Faith, hope, and love;
> But the greatest of them all is love."

Susan then rose to read the eulogy she and Eddy had written the night before. I had sat with them a few minutes and then left to be with Miguel in the living room.

Miguel was sitting with all of us and listening to his father's good deeds, his well-lived life. He heard nothing of himself, of his sisters in México, of his mother. His heart must have been split in two, as it had been since he'd left his mom to find his father. Tot was never going to give him what he wanted. There had to be so much anger hidden behind his sadness and his cheerful persona, but I had not yet seen it.

I turned to check on the children; they were asleep, cushioned on the hard pews with blankets and the loving bodies of their other mom and Maria Elena. They will not remember the touch of their abuelo's hand, the gentle smiles they exchanged in the year of life they shared with him. They will not miss him the way their cousins Rafael and Steven will. When I cry about him in years to come they will feel my sadness, not their own. He will be to them what my abuelos were to me: stories and unformed wishes.

I will tell them one day about the last time they saw their abuelo alive. Two months before his death, I will say, we had flown down for your Tía Sue's fortieth birthday party. That day the sun shone, as it does in Los Angeles in early autumn. Did you know it was el Día de Independencia for México? Yes, Mami, you will say, and roll your eyes. We know. Pues, que bueno. The party took place at a local park. I snapped a picture of your abuelo with a big grin on his gaunt face. Your abuela had dropped him off near the picnic tables. The pulmonary fibrosis meant walking exhausted him. He couldn't play with you, my rambunctious one-year-olds, and we had spent most of our time with your abuela at the swings while he sat in the shade.

Before that we had visited in June, at Rafael's eighth grade graduation. He and abuela had visited in July. We had taken every opportunity to join the familia down south with cheap Southwest fares, and you two were young enough to travel for free. When you are older, you will hear the rest. Or the rest I am willing to share.

Susan came down from the altar and sat down next to me, and I patted her leg. I dropped with the others on the kneelers, the motion helping me surrender any control I pretended to have. Resting my head on my hands, I closed my eyes.

"Go in peace, to love and serve the Lord."

"Thanks be to God." The words came back to me as if I said them every week at mass.

The casket rolled down the aisle and I walked behind with my family, cradling a sleeping Gina in her dark blue dress. I resisted the urge to turn and run back into the church and make it my sanctuary as I had as a girl. Within its heavy, gray walls, I had hidden my fears among the rituals, my moves choreographed as they hadn't been in years. I inhaled the pungent aroma of the incense before leaving the church.

Stepping into the sun outside, I saw León, my father's friend from México. I had fond memories of being a chamaca swimming in his pool in Guadalajara. He was the only person I remember visiting in México who knew Tot. His body, big for a Mexicano, shared the demeanor of a lion, chest out, deep voice greeting me. He sported his signature, pencil-thin moustache.

As I looked across his shoulder at the social hall, I recalled a picture of myself dancing with Tot for my eighth grade graduation. The photo was blurry, a result of my mom's lack of practice with my father's camera. He was forty-eight years old to my lucky thirteen. It was a moment of dulzura that was unusual between us. Bodies close, music and dance present. I was wearing an ankle-length turquoise dress my mother made. His curls were plastered down with hair product, mine were blown dry to gentle, soft waves. I did not know how to dance. The graduating class was half Latinos, but that father-daughter dance was a waltz and I struggled against his sure skill as a leader.

Moving toward the limo, I saw the one friend in attendance I claimed as mine. Meg, who I had known for fifteen years, hugged me in that understated way of hers, bodies held apart in the form of an A. Our friendship had sustained painful bruises, but we clung to the thread that defined us both—an unflagging loyalty to those we loved. A woven cloth hat covered her mostly hairless head, a few blond wisps surviving the chemotherapy. She looked even paler without hair, and her usual round figure was skinny, too similar to my father's. Her illness made me want to run. Instead, I asked after her health.

"I'm okay. One more set of chemo in the hospital over Thanksgiving weekend, and it should be clear sailing." She smiled in that brave way of hers I was borrowing for the day.

"I'll be back in LA then, so I can come see you. That's only three weeks away." My eye twitched again. I dreaded stepping inside another hospital. "Will you be up for visitors?"

"Oh, sure. I may not have bundles of energy, but a friendly face will help. I hate those gowns. So unladylike."

I searched her face for clues for how she really felt, but she was as stoic as my father. And today was not a day for me to plumb for more bad news. Meg wouldn't let on anyway. A woman of protocol, she had come for me, to offer her suffering body to my torn heart.

"How's Amalia?"

She smiled. "We are going to visit my family in Ohio over Christmas, celebrate the end of this horrible year. I want to spoil her rotten." She pushed her glasses back onto the bridge of her nose, looked around, and whispered conspiratorially: "That's a secret. Don't tell anyone it's my plan."

I hugged her frail frame one last time and joined my family in the limo. I sat between Miguel and Eddy, no interest in holding their hands or pondering what thoughts coursed through the minds of my two brothers as we were driven back to my parents' house.

9.
Pulling Away

WE FLOWED INTO MY PARENTS' LARGE BACK-
yard full of fruit trees, my father's pride. The gathering was subdued despite the sun reaching down to us
through the aguacate trees, the first avocados of the season hanging invitingly just beyond our reach.

"There is where he planted his fava beans, que no?"
Gloria pointed to a dry, hard patch of dirt.

"Yeah. Amazing to think they grew despite that soil!" I
said, a gardener myself. "Those fava beans were as determined as Tot."

"And over there," Eddy pointed to the chain link fence
separating our yard from our longtime neighbor, Pete's,
"he grew his lemongrass and ajo."

"Ay sí," my mother appeared, "I had to fight him for
space to plant my tomatoes."

She fell silent. "And now . . ." Her voice choked up.

I froze as her tears flowed freely, a dam I thought could
never spring a leak. Instinctively, I moved away from this
mom I did not know how to talk to and met Susan on the
patio leading into the kitchen.

"How do you think León found out about Tot all the
way in Guadalajara?" I asked.

Her forehead wrinkled and her mouth widened.
"What do you mean? Tot met him here when they were
waiters. One of their mutual friends called him," she said.

"I thought he was Tot's friend from before he came here."

Susan knew so much more about Tot's life. I walked slowly inside, making myself greet people, accept their hugs, and direct them to the backyard for food and drinks. I saw Tot's BB gun underneath the kitchen counter, his weapon for scaring the squirrels that ate his precious aguacates.

Fred's firm hand came down on my shoulder and I turned. His hair was graying and disappearing, but his good-humored grin remained constant. "Hey, Linda, do you know where your dad kept extension cords?"

I smiled, sure the spot hadn't changed over the years. Tot had a system for everything. "Yeah, I'll go get you one."

As I walked through Tot's den, I paused to touch his phone. The programmed names were all Mexicanos: Alfonso, Hugo, Memo, Moca. It was his private cultural circle even though my parents' social circle was mostly Colombianos.

Entering the dark garage, I felt around for the light switch. My dad's car, worktable, and well-used tools waited expectantly for hands to touch them again. The drawer required a strong yank to open, as it was packed to the brim with extension cords. I pulled one out, the neatly wrapped cord a trademark of my father, and unwound it. I noticed one of my father's most endearing and exasperating traits—the plug had broken, and Tot had devised a makeshift cardboard device to keep the prongs in place. Even I, a novice in all things electrical, knew this was dangerous. My father must have known this, but his penchant for fixing and reusing had won the battle that day.

My initial chuckle turned to anger. It was an unnecessary risk. He refused to throw it away because he hated to waste anything that might be repairable. I pulled out three "mended" sets until I found one I was willing to plug in without fear of sparks flying. I tossed the broken ones into the kitchen trash, brushing past Miguel as he balanced a pile of dirty plates and glasses.

Our eyes met. He had the look of the puppy who had entered this house twenty-two years ago, seeking attention from the man who had left him as a boy. I asked him to say a few words at an altar we had set up. His eyes watered, and a tear ran down a cheek reddened from working in the sun and grit of his demolition business. He nodded and ushered people into the living room.

As I surveyed the fifteen or so people seating themselves on the matching flowered loveseats and blue velour armchairs, I sensed my separation from them. These were people I had seen on and off most of my life until leaving for college, and yet I knew very little about them. Most had been adults in my childhood, most immigrants to my US nacimiento, most had settled into an uneasy limbo between their homeland and their adopted citizenship. Unlike my father, most had an audible accent, like my mother. These accents fell on my ears comfortably.

I slipped into my parents' room for a quiet moment, surveyed their furnishings. Nothing would tell you my father had little formal education, came from another country, and had stories he never meant to tell. The only culturally different adornment was the framed print of Our Lady of Perpetual Help, popular among Catholics. Mary had a grim look. Baby Jesus was looking away from his mom even though his hands were placed tenderly in one of hers.

Returning to the living room, I surveyed a low table holding memories of Tot's life with contributions placed on it by his children—his athleticism captured by a golf ball, a racquetball, and a soccer ball. My father had so much more to give me, and I couldn't begin to translate his attempts until now. He got me started playing soccer right when Title IX allowed for it. I became a lifelong sports fan. I cheered with him and my brother for the LA Rams in the days of the fearsome foursome.

Once, my father got us all tickets to ride on a bus with other Century Plaza Hotel workers to a Santa Barbara hotel. They were broadcasting the Rams in a game that was blacked out in LA. There we were, two kids with mostly immigrant Latino and European men, cheering for the Rams. He gave me permission to have the heart and drive of an athlete in an era when girls were discouraged from competing in anything.

My sister had ordered a cake decorated with miniature Mexican flags, mariachis and a plastic figurine of a dark man sitting in a chair watching TV. I fished out one of the extension cords from the trash and placed it by the remote control and Betamax tape. Lighting the velas, I slumped onto the floor, leaned my back against one of the velour chairs and closed my eyes, comforted by the low hum of voices. The mood was quiet but not austere, as if to buoy up my mom, who was not the bustling hostess we were all used to seeing flit among us.

Tot died on Día de los Muertos. A holiday I had learned about in this country and was "celebrating" for the first time, with my father as the main actor.

"We are here," Miguel said, "to say goodbye to Rosendo. This altar has memories of his life."

Listening to Miguel's sonorous voice, I surveyed the gathering. León had not come to the house. The men on Tot's automatic dial were missing. The only Mexican immigrant present was Miguel.

"We can share our memories now."

Miguel looked at me, but Susan spoke first. "Linda and I played soccer and other sports, and he expected us to go to college. He treated us the same as Eddy."

I would have said the same thing if she had not spoken so quickly. Miguel flinched but I couldn't hold his pain. I am sure others in the living room shared stories about Tot, but my mind pulled away from death's grasp. People trickled out slowly after we cut the cake and served it with café, leaving the family Tot had left behind to sort out his life.

&

My first morning back in Berkeley, as the early morning light appeared, I got up and wrapped myself in a blanket on the couch. The marigolds' scent on the altar was strong, but not strong enough to pull Tot's soul back to me. The velas burned unhurried near the plastic man watching TV. I had taken it from the altar in LA and slipped it surreptitiously into my suitcase before leaving my mom's house.

Opening my photo album and staring at pictures of my father over the last year, I looked for the clues he dropped, like breadcrumbs, to let me know he was leaving us. There he was holding Teo on this same couch during his last visit here, when his leg was swollen as big as an elephant's. He had declined my absurd invitation to take a leisurely walk around the block.

There was his mention of a book detailing the possible options for his declining lung capacity, his interest in my suggestion of seeing a naturopath, but with the unambiguous parameter that he fly back and forth in the same day. I think he wanted to make sure he died in LA.

I never arranged that appointment for him in Berkeley, never read the book or learned the name of his illness.

I never told Susan and Eddy that he had given me the papers. He had said I would need to make hard decisions, but I balked numerous times when action was required.

Where were those malditos papeles detailing his wishes? I didn't read them, just stuffed them in among my dirty clothes and took the envelope out when I unpacked. Walking to my office, I opened the file cabinet, and looked in the hanging folder marked "Important papers." They were easy to find in the manila envelope.

Returning to the living room, my body shook with sobs. Against every wish in my body, I opened my photo album and pulled out the last photo of him at Susan's birthday party. He was smiling, his brimmed hat doffed at the camera, his white hair like a halo, his brown skin contrasting with the white sweater that hung loosely on his dying body. Miguel was grinning on his right. Tot's heart had been beating in that picture. It had been beating when I started setting up this altar.

I got up and placed the picture gently next to Conchita, his mamá. My altar was complete.

10.
Sitting in the Muck

ON MY FIRST TRIP TO LA FOR CHRISTMAS WITH-out Tot, the kitchen smelled of loneliness and of the stale, musty bread in the wooden breadbox. My father would take the two loaves of their separate bread preferences, intertwine them, and re-pack them into the plastic bags. It must have sat there since his death, the interlocking he and she slices now coated in mold.

After throwing them out, I went to make a fresh, stronger pot of coffee for myself. My mom sat alone at the kitchen table, drinking her preferred pale brown coffee, rewarmed in the microwave.

Her mug bore a company logo from a hotel event, as Tot brought home whatever giveaways were left from corporate banquets. Once he had unhooked and taken crystals from an old chandelier they replaced at the hotel, which we promptly hung in our homes as prisms. Acquiring old computers from who knows where was his passion, and he passed them on to us, outdated models with minute amounts of memory and archaic operating systems. He was stuck in a paradigm that "if it's not completely broken, don't buy a newer version." I suppose it was his way of not letting the road get so easy that you forgot how to fend for yourself. Quién sabe.

"He looked at me when he was dying and said: 'What will you do without me?'" Mom said, leaving her café untouched, her long, ragged nails drumming a quiet dirge on the dining room table.

I had heard this line many times in the few months since his death and now saw the reality of his apprehension. To have my mom, who usually drove her internal engine in fourth gear, remain stuck in first or second, unnerved me. I didn't understand what it meant to lose someone you had slept next to for over forty years, thinking you had survived the worst.

"Oh, Linda. Nobody cares about me. Only Rosendo, and he's gone."

"Mom, that's not true. We love you."

"No me quieren. You're just saying that."

"Mom, you need to get out. Come back up north with us."

"I don wantu go."

"Mom, Gina and Teo need you. They want their abuela." The wobble in my voice joined her despair.

"No. Déjeme sola." Her shadow turned and stomped away. This was another dialog that repeated itself, her desolation only overridden with the anger with which she shielded herself as she surveyed a life without her viejo.

The next day as I lay on the den couch, Gina walked over to me clutching her fuzzy bear tightly. "Look, Mami, ouchie." I was unsuccessfully recovering from my sleepless night by catching the last inning of a baseball game where my Giants were beating the team I grew up listening to—the Dodgers.

"How sad, mija." I took Gina's little osito and gave it a big beso where she pointed. Pulling my Swiss Army knife out of my purse, I used the tiny scissors to cut the hanging thread.

I fingered the red surface of my knife cover; an unusual gift to give your grown daughter, although no more incongruous than the soccer cleats he bought me at fourteen rather than planning a quinceañera. I had put the knife on my Christmas list maybe seven years ago.

Eddy pulled his gift out of my pile after I opened Tot's knife. "I got you a Swiss Army knife too, but he actually bought your gift this year," Eddy said. "I'll get you something else." He knew, as I did, that our mom did most of the gift buying, and Tot's decision to buy it sprang from his oft-hidden heart.

"All better," I said as I closed up the scissors.

Gina looked at me for a minute and then pointed to my face. "Mami ouchie?"

I frowned. I didn't have any ouchies. Walking to the bathroom, I looked at my countenance. The splotches on my cheeks and forehead had darkened over the last month, like I had put on sunscreen with a cavalier swipe of my hand, missing whole parts of my face. Stress ouchies, sprouting when Tot died.

Gina ran over to Teo, who was fitting triangles and squares into the holes of a plastic cube and showed him her "healed" mascota. He looked up briefly and nodded, pushing hard on the triangle, his tongue sticking out between his lips as it did when he was concentrating. Their sweet voices were like salve on my tired heart, coating it every day as they discovered a new word or squealed with delight when batting around a balloon.

I closed my eyes, taking in the recent energy of this house. Retirement meant he no longer had to smile and attend to both his boss and his guests' every wish. Spending more time with his grown children, he took notice of who we were apart from what he wanted us to be. It had been a tough transition for all of us. He asked more questions and observed more before commenting. Tot also saw that mom served as the intermediary between him and their children. She guarded this role fiercely, even as she resented the burden because she so rarely liked the news we conveyed to her.

As he had slowly become accustomed to life at home, a sense of relief permeated his activities. He slept more, often in his recliner in the den. They both loosened the reins of their work ethic and settled into an energetic yet flexible rhythm. With us gone, the house was big enough to give them their own corners.

My mom's domain was concentrated in the kitchen, where she prepared meals for a grateful Tot. A stovetop chemist, she used her hands and taste buds to concoct delicious, healthy meals that would, in a restaurant review, be dubbed a "Mexican–Colombian–American–Chinese" fusion. My father became a waiter and busboy again, setting the table and cleaning up the trastes.

They both tended the garden with the help of a gardener who came by once a month to mow and prune. My father planted his fava beans every year and watered the avocado, lemon, orange, plum, and peach trees. My mom cultivated her wide array of flowers, including rose bushes, fuchsias, white gardenias, and calla lilies. She often painted her homegrown bouquets after placing them in a vase. Mom had always been an artist. Even when we were in grammar school she had taken art classes. I remember a picture of Eddy she reproduced from his school photo and sketches she made of us. Her art was stark, and somewhat abstract with thicker lines, less detail.

Tot's retreat was the den housing his air popcorn machine, huge TV, brown lounger, and small cabinet full of meticulously labeled VHS and Betamax tapes. His first VCR was a Beta, and he was a loyal man. When they became obsolete, he refused to let his go, although he bought a newer model to tape videos for his youngest grandchildren.

"Remember to take them with you the next time you drive down," he would say to me.

Happier than he had ever been, he was also sicker, cutting down his physical activities so slowly we could discount it.

My mother's voice echoed my concern, complaining her viejo was always durmiéndose en el den. "He's always poofed," she said, using one of her Spanglish word scrambles. "He doesn't help me much anymore."

Neither of us had stopped to ball our qualms into one big wad of terror.

❧

Now we were all wandering in the valley of death, figuring out how to live without Tot. To add to my grief, Meg's sister had called a few hours before we drove down. Meg, who I visited in the hospital during my Thanksgiving visit, had collapsed during her December visit with family. The doctors found her tumor had spread to her brain. She died soon after I sent her a letter.

> Meg,
>
> I am writing out what I hopefully already said to you.
>
> What is so hard for me about my father's death is that we couldn't say goodbye. I couldn't ask him to tell me why he left a family in México or what his greatest lesson in life had been. All the richness of his silence was left . . .

I know you're depressed and totally unable to maintain the illusion of control we all so dearly protect. Nevertheless, there are days to be lived yet and you and I (as well as you and many others) have what my father and I didn't: a chance to say and ask, rant and rave.

Let me help if I can, this is one of your last chances to boss me around (a gift I bestow on an elite few—you and Gina and Teo). If it feels better to you, it would help me enormously in my healing/grief process around my dad.

You asked me several years ago where I stood with faith and how and to whom we go for healing. I was thinking today that I need to watch *Harold and Maude* soon. If faith exists in me, it is in the spirit of Maude. That woman, or character, if you will, suffered! And yet she emerged from that suffering. Literally. She emerged. Can you feel that? She lived as who she was, even if it stretched our boundaries and good taste.

You sent me a card many moons ago with a quote from Adrienne Rich on what constitutes an honorable human relationship. You are one of those people who have gone the hard way with so many of us.

When friends held a memorial for Meg in January, I could not muster my heart to go, fearful I would sob hysterically with the weight of loss.

ॐ

"Linda." Six months later, Susan's call got me off the couch in Berkeley. "I found Mom drugged and woozy, probably from the anti-depressants."

I flew to LA. Susan had driven Mom to the Kaiser hospital where Tot had died. It was late April, a day before Tot's birthday. Mom stayed overnight for observation and was released in the morning. We met with her and a therapist later that afternoon.

We love you, mom... So what... Now, Mrs. González, your daughters are worried about you... They wouldn't have put me in the hospital if they cared, que desgracia, people know me here... Mom! You didn't answer the doorbell and couldn't get up... So what, I lost Rosendo, who cares? ... We're worried about you, mom... Why did you embarrass me in front of Virginia? ... Mrs. González, I'm sure she was concerned, like your daughters said... You don't know, these people talk... Mom, you still have us... You don't want me, nobody wants me, I don't want to be alive... Oh, Mom... Mrs. González, I hear your daughters saying they do want you... They don't want me; they are too busy.

The fifty-minute therapy spin cycle came to a halt and we drove to Mar Vista in silence.

Embarrassment rose in my throat, followed by anger at Mom for caring more about what others would think than believing we loved her. This morphed into rage at the therapist for her passive interventions that left us sitting alone in the muck.

My mother slumped in the passenger seat, her eyes closed, her chin sagging and full of pelitos, her hair showing at least an inch of gray before the brown kicked in. She fingered a penny she had picked up on the sidewalk. Mom used to go gambling in Las Vegas two to three times a year, coming home gleeful about the money she'd won on the slot machines while others had lost theirs. Ana Dilia had invited her to go the following weekend but she had said no. Her spirit hovered between heaven and earth, and no amount of tugging on her heartstrings pulled her back to us. She had resolved to never win again.

I touched what was becoming my recurring wish, the one that agreed with hers: "I wish my mom was dead." It was not a cruel wish. It was one to reconcile her outsides to her insides, to acknowledge the death of her belief in the goodness inside her, crushing her ability to see it in me or in the ones I loved. To survive she had created and worn a series of masks, masks that had become glued to her soul and had left the genuine pieces of her difficult to access.

I thought we had outwitted that old abandonment wound, thought our patient love made a difference. Opening the car door for her after arriving, she waved off my outstretched hand. Kissing Susan goodbye, I reluctantly followed Mom inside and walked straight through the house to the backyard, to sit in the swing under the biggest of the avocado trees and gather my feelings.

This tree produced a type of aguacate that is not typical for California. They were called "Fuerte" because they survived the 1913 freeze after being brought from México. Maintaining their green color when ripe, the buttery-flavored fruit is susceptible to disease due to its thin skin. They were once the gold standard in California, only to be displaced in the 1930s by the Hass avocado because of its thicker skin.

I leaned back to look at the few remaining leaves rustling in the soft breezes of April. It was spring and their season was over.

&

Mom's nostalgia belied the reality of her complex relationship to Tot over forty years. Sitting at the kitchen table with Tot one day during a visit from college, I scanned the local newspaper as Mom bustled around the stove, chopping chicken into small bits with a cleaver, tossing snow peas and carrots into a hot wok with a delicious aroma of sesame oil and garlic.

"Ay no. Can't you make me something else tonight?" said Tot, sniffing the spices that told him carne asada was not on the menu.

"Don't be so stubborn, viejo," said Mom, bringing him café and a blueberry muffin. "You know you like it. It's better than the China Palace—too greasy there."

Taking a jab at his favorite restaurant was like a picador shoving a lance between a bull's shoulders. "What a pendeja you are," said Tot, grabbing the muffin and putting the whole thing in his mouth. "You can't cook better than los Chinos."

"Pues, you can't cook!" Her hands moved rapidly, the loud sizzle of the wok matching the mood shift, turning their sharp banter into a battle of fierce wills, mixing Spanish and English as they had since I was a young girl.

Their harsh tone had always bothered me, as much a part of my life as the wooden table we were sitting at.

"Ay, vieja. You think you are so right, like all women." He chuckled and slurped his café loudly. "And you didn't put enough milk in. Que asco."

The barb aimed at my mother singed me. He expected me to join in his ridicule by laughing; I stared at him. He looked at me, eyes narrowing when I remained silent.

Eddy's view of our parents' complexities is almost the mirror opposite. He remembers Mom mocking Tot and telling him to stop if he were silly or too emotional. He heard Tot tell her, "I was the child without a childhood." It was as if he were saying "I'm finding the child myself now as an older person."

Susan's view was a combination of both of ours. If she cried, Tot made fun of her. If she got mad, they laughed at her. She shut down because she didn't feel safe with either one of them. As she reflected on this, her final words were: "Isn't that sad? That's so sad."

Throughout the years, we wove in and out of the inevitable word jousts in my mother's kitchen, each of us reaching different decisions about them and ourselves. This pattern of shutting down emerged more fully after Tot died, each one of us alone in our particular nightmare, one that didn't go away upon opening our eyes each morning.

꒰꒱

While the twins napped later that day, I helped Mom clean out Tot's clothes, my new plan to help her re-group. I had just pocketed some of his panuelas to take home with me when she handed a vest to me.

"Toma," she said.

I fingered the soft beige wool I had knit for him several years before—it was thick, because Tot, like the rest of us, was friolento. I chuckled at all the failed knitting projects that littered my path before I had learned to read a pattern and buy the right size needles and the right weight yarn. My rudimentary knowledge of knitting came from my mom, who did not follow patterns and did not have the patience to be a teacher. I figured out early on to either get it quick or get lost.

"Y éste también." She handed me a black vest.

"I knit that for you." Emboldened by my success with Tot's vest, I had found a more complicated pattern with plaited stitches for Mom.

"Well, I don't wear it."

Her words ripped at the already tender skin of my heart. She had sewn clothes for me as a girl and I hadn't liked the styles, but I had done my best to be grateful. I grabbed the vest and walked out of the room, holding it across my chest with both arms, feeling the dense softness against my short, angry breaths.

I escaped to the den and fell into Tot's soft brown recliner, automatically turned on his first generation big screen TV with the failing picture. It was like there was a light coating of sugar glaze on the screen, not bad enough for my dad to invest in a new TV.

Tot's energy permeated the den, his many eyes watching me from the framed pictures of him with celebrities he served at the hotel—Lee Trevino, Johnny Carson, Freddie Prinze, Sr., Barbara Eden, and Tommy Lasorda, the long-time Dodgers manager.

❧

Standing up, I looked at him in the pictures, trying to see him as someone other than my dad. He was short and brown. I hadn't considered him that way before. What was it like for a self-educated immigrant working in an environment full of cigarette smoke and monstrous egos?

To distract myself, I pulled out the glass cleaner and

wiped his pictures one by one, the coat of grime trans-ferred from the glass to my cloth, for to feel my grief was to watch the stars fall from the sky and wonder if dawn would appear again on the horizon.

How did I miss seeing my father's role in our fam-ily, especially as he sickened over the last year? I flipped through the channels, my fingers imitating his. I had often joined him in the small den to watch sports rather than sidle up to my mom in the kitchen. I enjoyed the well-defined winners and losers. I might have wanted to be a homecoming princess, but my fiery temper was more at home cheering for my teams and playing soccer. He wel-comed me, while my mom had no interest in showing me how to cook arroz con pollo o chilaquiles.

Tot often shunned nice clothes for holidays and more formal occasions, tightening his pants with a belt that was too big, too old, and too ridiculous. The belt had survived several decades. When he lost weight, he added holes, let-ting the longer end flop down. If we complained too much, he would sometimes cut part of it off, leaving a rough edge. My mom, while annoyed at him, ignored social conven-tions in her own way, stirring her coffee with the handle of a nearby knife, sticking a wet spoon in the sugar bowl, and eating food off someone else's plate.

When Tot died, it could have been a transformational moment for my mom. She could have re-energized her-self and become the abuela and mom we had known her to be. Yet, something fundamental in her heart died with Tot. She folded, pushed her cards towards the dealer and walked away from the table of la vida. She had given up so much to stay with this man, and now he had left her alone: her worst fear. My mom became a bitter shadow, her face unsmiling as I leaned in to kiss her on each visit, her wrinkled cheek grudgingly receiving my beso.

૨૦

Teo developed a bad cough a few weeks after my first Father's Day without Tot, and the racking sound singed me with the memories of my last phone call with him. We gave him liquid albuterol, but it didn't ease his labored breathing. The advice nurse recommended taking him to the hospital. I bundled him up in his jacket and drove the five minutes to Children's Hospital in a daze, not wanting to take on doctors who might resist our alternative health care approach. My watch read three a.m.

When I opened the backdoor of the car, Teo was asleep, the rattle quieter. Feeling thankful to avoid a visit to the hospital, I drove back home.

Carolyn heard the car pull in and ran out. "Why are you back?"

I pointed to Teo. "Look—he's sleeping."

"Linda, he's really sick. You have to take him to the hospital."

I didn't believe her. He had never taken a prescription drug before the albuterol we gave him that night. Driving back reluctantly, I carried him inside, his head nestled in the crook of my neck, the rattle in his chest stronger.

The nurse looked at him and said, "He's having an asthma attack. We need to admit him. Is this the first time?"

"Yes. How can you tell?" I stroked his curly hair and held back the accusations gathering steam inside me for being such a fool with my baby's health at risk.

"See his neck, how the skin puckers in when he tries to breathe? It is a sure sign he's not getting enough oxygen. He's working really hard to breathe."

I looked at him with such love and fear I thought my heart would melt into a pool of butter. The nurse put an oxygen mask on his small mouth and nose. I held him gently, watching the indentations go in and out, in and out, until they gradually disappeared. An hour later I snuggled with him, wrapping myself around him like a wool cobija, gingerly pushing the little oxygen tubes in his nose when he fought to pull them out.

Drifting in and out of sleep, I promised to not close my eyes and heart to danger again. My son. My father. My mother. I had to get a grip. What was I doing in this hospital, so exhausted and so afraid?

11.
Full and Empty

I FLEW TO SAN ANTONIO A MONTH LATER IN JULY 1997 and joined a group of multicultural consultants at a remote ranch surrounded by a desert full of sunset colors. It was the first flight I had taken in a long time that didn't involve death or a crisis. Carolyn's mom had had a serious stroke a few months before the twins were born so we had begun negotiating trips to moms who had left their best years behind them.

Late on Saturday afternoon, Jo, the Transactional Analysis trainer, led us through a visualization exercise. She asked us to remember our earliest encounter with someone of a different race. Closing my eyes and concentrating, I waited. After about a minute my breathing became shallow, my legs squeezed together, and my fingers clutched the top of my knees. No scene emerged—I had failed the test. Listening with half an ear as others shared painful memories that had marked them for life, I wanted to bolt from the room.

She turned to me. "You've been quiet. What is going on?" Jo had dark eyes that telegraphed the message: "Nothing gets by me."

I remained silent.

"How do you identify culturally?" she asked, folding dark brown hands on her lap and gazing at me.

"Good question," is all I could muster. And then a little girl's plaintive, embarrassed cry: "I lost my culture." My words stood stark and lonely. I licked the salty tears on my face and accepted the tissue someone handed me.

"I knew you were smart," Jo said after I blew my nose and relaxed back into my chair. "I now see your deep heart."

An African American woman approached me at the break. "I know how you feel. I feel the same."

I looked at her dreads, her African batik dress, and recalled her contributions to the discussion. To believe her was to believe in a hope I had not watered in years.

Susan had teasingly called me a born-again Latina. The kids attended Centro Vida pre-school, I dressed them in Mexican and Guatemalan outfits, and bought the Ibarra brand of Mexican hot chocolate, singing "bate, bate, chocolate" as it melted into the rice milk. My barriers were wearing down as my children softened the sharp edges of my own childhood.

❧

Almost ten years passed before I recalled an early encounter with someone of a different race. I was five years old and finishing first grade at Monte Vista Elementary School before moving to Mar Vista. Whenever Mrs. Walkey said something about second grade, I prodded her: "Do you know I'm not coming back?"

"Yes, Linda, I know."

She did not pronounce my name like my family did, and there was no regret in her tone. I enjoyed school, felt smart and in my element in an all-English environment. She asked me to read to the whole class one day while she did errands. I sat down happily on the wooden stool in the front of the class while a parent watched.

I don't remember the book. What I remember was the parent unnecessarily clueing me when a difficult word came up. I worried the kids would think I didn't know the word. But I didn't stand up for myself and tell her to stop. I was not allowed to be so smart, not with a name like González in a classroom filled with Smiths and Murphys.

Each time someone looked over my shoulder or doubted my words, my brilliance fought with my vergüenza. For years, I feared I would be found out to be a fake, my accomplishments shining stars that belonged to someone else, someone more deserving than me.

I remembered Gloria's story about how Tot reacted to her grades and how she felt her efforts were never good enough. I understood why he had told her, and then me, we could have gotten all A's. We had misinterpreted his message because of his stern delivery. He was telling us we were capable of being the very best.

When I graduated from high school, there was a big awards banquet. My dad set up a tripod to take pictures and I thought, "He thinks I'm going to get something. How embarrassing if I don't." They called my name once and I felt relieved. They then called my name several more times, and I was embarrassed for the opposite reason—it was too much and set me apart from others when I had tried so hard to blend in.

I am not sure my mom totally aligned with Tot's under-lying message. She knew the more we achieved, the fur-ther it exposed her gaps. A picture of Mom, Tot, Eddy and me together at my college graduation in 1982 revealed the snags in their expectations. I wore a sash protesting the decision to deny tenure to a feminist professor, ruining any pomp and circumstance from my cap and gown.

"Come on, Linda, take it off," my mom said.

I ignored her, too caught up in my attempts to find a tribe, opting for the feminists. I refused to hold hands with my two cultures that day.

Mom whispered in my ear as we entered Memorial Church where the English degree students were gathering: "Couldn't you have gone to a less expensive school?"

Her words scorched me like a tortilla left on the flame too long. I had inadvertently overshot the mark, which had been to graduate from college, but not from one where we stood next to moneyed families. This caste system encircled me, caught within privilege and deprivation simultaneously, full and empty.

My mother had fought her fear of being a failure all her life. This doubt had been sown before she met my father and had lain in wait until his death. It then grabbed her by the tail and tossed her into her worst nightmare.

ॐ

I attended a follow-up training after San Antonio, held at the San Francisco Zen Center. Our homework included reading an article about the many layers of sadness; a surge of emotion knocked the air out of my lungs. I raised my hand, wanting and not wanting to transform the knot inside my body into words.

"I didn't just lose my father, I lost any chance to ask him about his life, his culture, his history." My body sank down into the chair, weary from fighting to keep myself together.

One of the facilitators, a Cuban immigrant named Hilda, looked at me with compassion born from her own experiences of heartache and loss. "You can still ask him."

Not able to hold her gaze, I looked through narrowed eyes at her mala, the brown smooth beads moving gently between her slender, café con leche fingers. I didn't believe her, overwhelmed with the bleakness in which my mother now lived.

Another gust of wind rattled my delicate bearings on the third day of the workshop.

"I judge my mom by what I suppose a mom and a widow should be. She can't do anything but fail," I said ruefully.

"What are those standards?" asked Hilda.

"You know, the June Cleaver I grew up watching—always pleasant, having a wise word for me when I stumble, calm under stress, aguantando for the sake of her children."

I managed a smile at expectations I didn't even believe. This revelation broke through some of my resentment toward my mom, and at the break I sat outside in the sun with a cup of manzanilla in my hands. What if I quit thinking love could be measured, like my parents had taught me?

I could only approach this possibility with trepidation, like I did the Grapevine on the I-5, a steep climb up and over Tejon Pass. This part of the highway coiled up the mountain and signaled the homestretch, only one hundred miles from Los Angeles. It was the hardest part of the journey. To stop measuring love would require my same undivided attention.

12.
Tempting Fate

IN FEBRUARY OF 1998, SUSAN TOLD ME MIGUEL'S mother had died in México. It was our weekly check-in about Mom. She mentioned it near the end of the conversation.

"It was unexpected. He went down to México last week."

"Do you think it's okay to call him?"

"I don't know. He was pretty abrupt on the phone." Her voice carried the same combination of anger and exasperation it often held when speaking about Miguel. Her personality contained virgo tendencies that did not mix easily with Miguel's exuberant aquarian persona.

Supporting the phone on my left shoulder, I kept matching tiny, multicolored socks in pairs, hoping the dryer had mysteriously swallowed only one or two.

"He rarely talked about his mom," said Susan.

Susan's comment made me drop down into the meaning of this death. It didn't touch me initially, because I had never let Miguel's other family exist other than as a distant island on the horizon. With my mom's ongoing depression, I had even less interest in finding more sadness in my heart. I didn't even know the name of Tot's first wife who he abandoned.

"Miguel was used to keeping Tot's secrets," I said. "We all kept silent, when you think about it."

I said goodbye, collected the sock bundles, and carried them to the twins' room. Sitting down on the colorful alphabet squares that cushioned their falls, I envied the innocence of their lives. This room held growth and possibility while all around me the elders were dying.

❧

The last time I visited Los Angeles, I had gone to eat lunch with Miguel at Don Chuys, one of Tot's favorite restaurants. Miguel leaned forward after we had ordered and showed me his gold bracelet. The plate that joined the links said 'Rosendo'. I looked at him with shock, having thought Miguel was his name. He said that when he came to visit nuestro papá for the first time, Tot refused his hug, saying, "I have another son with my name. You have to change yours."

Miguel at the airport, eager to greet Tot, ready to forgive, ready to begin anew. His smile and abrazo met with a grim face and outstretched hand. Tot couldn't bear the sight of his son's hunger because it reminded him of all he had locked away to survive. His head must have hurt that day, his mind flooded with images of Teresita , of the look on her face when he made it bien claro he was coming to the US with or without her. He had done what he thought needed to be done so he could take his place in a world that wanted to thwart his aspirations.

There are many things I could have said when Miguel showed me his bracelet, but I kept silent. Miguel's voice became the rapid-fire of a machine gun, trying to get the words out swiftly, distracting himself from the searing pain of my father's words.

"I picked Miguel Angel like the archangel."

It would have been better if Miguel had demanded something of me to shake up my malaise, but he just handed me this information like a plate of burnt cookies. I took one to be polite.

The name stories in our family were both provincial and bizarre. My mom said my dad named us. Susan was the fifth most popular name for US born babies in 1956, and Linda was the third most popular name in 1958. Nevertheless, he could have picked Karen or Debra or Patricia, knowing Linda was part of his eldest daughter's name. Given he picked Rosendo for both sons, I really couldn't complain.

"What's happening with your son Brandon?" I asked, moving from one bothersome topic to another, "We haven't seen him for a while."

"Lydia lo llevó a Arizona. I haven't seen him. She won't give me their address."

"You're his father and you pay child support. They have to tell you," I said.

"I asked the people at the office but they said they couldn't tell me," he responded.

"That doesn't make sense," I said.

"He knows where I am. He can come find me."

I shook my head at this pain pattern. We had not seen Brandon since he was nine. I had thought for years that Brandon was my father's eldest grandchild, born a few months before Rafael. But he was my father's sixth grandchild.

"Does Eddy know about you changing your name?" I asked.

"I don't know."

"Does Susan?"

"Yes. I told her a few years ago."

He admitted he hadn't married for love but to get the protection of legal residency. He had asked Tot to help him with immigration, and Tot said it would be difficult because my mom had to sign as well. Miguel stayed quiet; he didn't know how it all worked, he only knew our father was not stepping forward. He believed it was because Tot would then have had to explain why Miguel's legal name was Rosendo Manrique and his was Rosendo González.

After Tot said no to helping him with immigration, Miguel felt disillusioned. Everyone told him Tot had not behaved like a father, and now he wondered if he had been wrong to come find him. Miguel had cried in the arms of Lydia, his girlfriend. His rage grew and he slammed his fist into a window and cracked it, committed to his belief that no one would ever help him.

Lydia, who was in her early twenties, offered to marry him, and they arranged a civil ceremony. She was pregnant, which he didn't know at the time. Miguel received residency status, but thirty years later had not applied for citizenship. In his head, he was going to return to México.

But the question that lingered for Miguel was why his father could not darle su mano. Even now, years later, he repeated this question of why my father didn't help him. As if the answer would come, even though my father had been dead several years.

There was one time that Tot did protect him. Miguel was accused of being with a minor, a young woman not yet eighteen. He had dated her four months and was embarrassed to be seen with her because she was so much taller. Her mother found out and accused him of being with a minor. She testified in court that she had told Miguel she was nineteen so she could go out with an older man. He never went to jail and only paid a fine for a misdemeanor. That was when nuestro papá, my mom, and Susan went to court for him.

Susan remembered the incident as an accusation of indecent exposure. Even though Tot told her Miguel was not anybody to be trusted and had made bad mistakes, she and my mom went to court to testify he was with them during the alleged incident. I asked her why she did it. She smiled bitterly and reminded me she was young and Tot was telling her Miguel didn't do this, and she had to testify he was with them.

We walked to our respective cars, I hugged him good-bye, and drove quietly to my sister's house.

᪣

I asked Eddy later if he knew about the double naming. He did. He saw this as a sign of Tot's stubbornness, his unconscious denial of Miguel's existence by giving his second son the same name. It placed Eddy in an odd position—he didn't want to lose his name any more than Miguel did. From a selfish point of view, Eddy was glad Miguel changed his name, but Tot didn't ask him what he wanted as the other Rosendo. It was Tot's standard fait accompli approach.

With Miguel's arrival, my dad had to explain him to Mom. He decided to say Rosalinda was not his daughter, and trust Miguel was going to keep his mouth shut about his two sisters. Tot knew his son would do anything to keep him close. After his first meal with Miguel, my father must have pulled away from the curb and battened down his heart, locked his jaw, and prepared his story for Mom.

Part 3:
Change

Miguel's fifty-first birthday lunch with niece Joanna and
sisters Tere and Rosita at Chapultepec Park, México, D.F., 2001

Three sisters with Joanna at Teotihuacan, México, 2001

13.
Truth Thaws Your Defenses

TOT WAS DEAD, MIGUEL WAS ALIVE AND PARENT-less. My own waves of ongoing grief opened me to his. I called Miguel with trepidation. My Spanish was weakest in these delicate conversations where fear and ignorance collided. "¿Como estás?"

"Pues, better than Rosita." Miguel recounted his older sister's distress at losing both her parents so close together.

I thought of Tot's will and trust. There had been nothing in it for Miguel. Nothing. An awkwardness seeped into my bones; we were speaking as if his family in México had been a topic of conversation all along. In twenty-five years, I hadn't asked him even one question about his mother. There was one I had to ask, even if it brought my shame to a boiling point.

"Your mamá—What is her name?"

"Teresita del nino Jesús Durand de Manrique," he replied.

"I will light a candle for her."

"Okay, hermanita. I love you. Give a hug and kiss to the children."

I walked back to my office. After Tot died I had taken the photo from Susan's birthday, cropped out Miguel, and mailed a framed version to the four of us on the first Father's Day without him. It sat on my desk.

"You abandoned your wife and children." I said it out loud.

"*You can still ask him.*" Hilda had said this at the training and I wanted to believe her.

The Tot I missed so much, who had taught me fairness and honor, had failed me. I was ready to face it as I couldn't when I was sixteen or even thirty-eight, when I knew sin duda he had three children and another wife. I blew my nose with one of Tot's old white pañuelos and wandered outside, standing in front of the apricot tree that some friends had gifted me when he died.

"You abandoned your wife and young children."

"You abandoned me."

My father had been fascinated with The Man of La Mancha. He had miniature wooden statues of Don Quixote and Pancho and loved the "Impossible Dream," adding his voice to Robert Goulet's, exaggerating his tone like an opera singer to croon of the impossible dream, of bravery, of righting wrongs and reaching stars.

Immigrant made good, living the agreeable life while his first family struggled to explain la mancha of no father in the house. This was his maldita secret, and he was not here to help me bandage the gaping wound where my innocence and loyalty had once pulsed.

"*There are no problems, there are only situations.*" His voice resonated in the air around me, one of his favorite dichos mocking him and me.

"I disagree!" I yelled at the tree. "I disagreed with you as a child and I still do. Some things stink. Me da asco."

I had concentrated on my needs, as if we were still little children clamoring for Tot's precious love, the glue no longer holding us together. Now it only kept us stuck to lies. I couldn't lay it all at Tot's feet. I had been an adult for most of the time Miguel lived in the US. Each curve in my family was opening me up to another. I had served homeless strangers soup and listened to their woes on skid row rather than honestly deal with my own flesh and blood brother. After Tot died, I had hidden behind my grief and motherhood.

I opened the worm box and began scooping out some of the rich, dark soil to add to my vegetables and flowers.

"Mami?" Teo was standing at the top of the stairs.

"Ay, mi amor. Come and see what I am doing."

I ran up the steps and scooped him up, feeling his trusting arms around my neck. After setting him down in the grass, he leaned into the worm box and grabbed a worm.

"You need to put it back in a few minutes, querido."

"No, the worm is my sweetie."

I smiled, remembering that yesterday he had held a roly-poly bug in that same small hand and said, "That's my sweetie pie."

After washing our hands, we nestled in to watch Plaza Sésamo with Gina and munch on Goldfish, our favorite snack.

I told Gina I had been putting compost into the garden to feed the plants. She looked at me and said: "But flowers don't have mouths."

"Es verdad. They eat through their roots!"

Their comments prompted me to start a journal for both twins that night to capture all their wit and wisdom. Each entry brought joy amid the losses.

❦

Eddy remembered Miguel entering our sphere as a slow process, all of us gradually accepting his presence after the first unpleasant dinner. Mom was the most hostile toward him, and even she gradually eased up. In her better moments, she was almost kind to him.

Home videos and slides show us jumping into pools, standing before Angel Falls in Yosemite waving, walking among colonial style buildings in México, and delightedly hugging our new blonde dolls in front of the Christmas tree. Tot was a prolific photographer, and our home contained neatly categorized Kodak boxes with slides. His visual recording of our family dwindled as we reached our teens.

It was as if Tot had fulfilled his role. He abandoned our upbringing to people he thought knew more than he did about what we needed. All in silence. I didn't see the cords being cut, only unconsciously watched and learned my parents' lessons from their actions.

Be proud of your culture but don't talk about it.

Follow your dreams but make sure they are socially acceptable.

Get a good education but make sure it doesn't cost too much.

Look for love in your marriage but don't marry someone with less education or social standing.

Smile at the white people but don't trust them.

Don't forget where you came from but remember you are better than that now.

Speak Spanish but not outside the home.

You are never too good to take any kind of job, but remember you are made for better things.

With that as a backdrop, it is no wonder we kept Miguel at bay. He was in several Christmas pictures, his ready, earnest smile belying the fact that he got one gift from "all of us," no matter how often he brought us separate gifts. He must have been with his family in México when he was not with us, but we never asked.

Family secrets are like home repairs—you think you're just replacing the bath faucet and then the tile removal reveals wood rot and leaky pipes. Water seeps into the foundation and, over time, the integrity of what you rested your life on cracks. Further damage is inevitable without addressing the underlying problem. It requires excavation.

I dredged up more stories over the next weeks as the third anniversary of Tot's death approached. We had all heard different versions of a story with the underlying message that Miguel was forced to come here because of some problem with the law.

Eddy's recollection is that Tot's friend Alfonso told him, basically, "No vas a poder" with Miguel. He's a cohete, a firecracker. It influenced Eddy's thinking because it told him Tot's view of the whole Mexican family, not just Miguel. "You're just going to cope poorly with this situation, so you might as well leave it all behind."

There were other stories Eddy got directly from Miguel, who said nobody messed with him because he was the toughest guy on the block. He'd tell Eddy his adventures, like when he was attacked by three guys in a restaurant and used a curtain pole like a staff to fend them off. He would then go back to lamenting that he had to pay his dues and be humble.

There was a flavor to Miguel's reputation that resonated with Tot's stories of his own youth, according to Eddy. Tot was likely the youngest of his group of friends and had the least social status. From the few stories Tot shared with him, Eddy got the sense they were young and crazy guys seeking adventures. They would pretend Arturo was El Matador, a bullfighter would attract women.

One time they paid for a bull and corral. Arturo stepped into a very small Grade C bullfighting ring with some bleachers around it. Tot and Alfonso were his picadors. The bull was released, and the first thing he did was hook Alfonso under his horns, throwing him up into the seats. They laughed and said grandmas were beating him with their umbrellas: "Get off me, get off me!"

Miguel's flamboyance irked Tot because it brought up the past he had buried. He expected Miguel to change his ways as he had. Tot made Miguel go through penance, according to Susan, because he felt Miguel was irresponsible in México. She felt Tot's attitude with him was the same as with us: we must learn to take care of ourselves or he was not going to help us.

Plaza Sésamo was ending, with Lola and Pancho singing one last ditty and my queridos nodding their heads with the song's melody, half-smiles playing on their lips. They jumped off the couch and were soon involved in building a nest with blankets and pillows under the dining room table.

My lingering resistance thawed. After my initial focus of what Miguel lost, I surveyed what we had missed.

"I lost my culture."

I sat in the murky dregs of shame and guilt for several days. One Saturday, in the midst of giving the bougainvillea a drastic pruning, my mood lifted. I couldn't change the past and, in fact, I knew little about it. But what I did know is that I wanted desperately to rise to this challenge and find glue strong enough to repair the cracks in our family's foundation.

Tot was dead. Miguel was alive. I kept coming back to this.

14.
You Are My Hermano

THE NEXT DAY I CALLED SUSAN.

"I've been thinking about Miguel and how it must be for him. We can't do this half-brother crap anymore." I swallowed and kept talking. "At some point, we have to deal with our sisters, but we need to start here."

"I don't know how," she said, her own voice quavering, "and since Fred left, I don't have extra time or energy."

"I know. I'll figure something out."

She and Fred had separated the day after Christmas more than a year before. I was in shock when they told me, Fred and I hugging and crying in the kitchen he had so carefully remodeled to include both their wants. It broke my heart to see them in such misery. They still loved each other, and their sons were, as all children, struggling to understand the rift.

Susan had moved with the boys, now fifteen and ten, into an apartment, the four-plex my parents owned. My sister had had home births in two other apartments in the complex. Susan and Fred had moved there each time a crisis hit their family. Their last stay had been after they were robbed twice within months and had reluctantly sold their house. They had offered me shelter many times over the years when I was between housing and job transitions, and I dearly wished I could extend them the same kindness. I stayed in closer touch and made room in my heart for another casualty of the strain in my family.

"Susan," I paused. "I know how much you do, and I haven't done enough over the years. And now with Fred gone and Mom's depression, it's even tougher."

We both sniffled, licking our wounds, each other's silhouette scarcely visible across the valley between us.

"Mom's meaner with me living in her apartments, because the renters come to me when she forgets something they asked for. And she doesn't pay attention to the rents. I have to make sure they get collected and deposited."

"Mom isn't getting better. Can you come up for the kids' Centro Vida graduation? We only see each other when there's a crisis."

"Thanks. I'll think about coming up, but I feel overwhelmed," said Susan.

"Love you."

"Love you, too."

One magical day, Susan and I had given up expecting Mom to tell us she loved us, and we had begun to tell each other. Growing up, "I love you" was never said by our parents in English or Spanish. I had sought that cariño outside my home, from neighbors, teachers, and religious retreats where crying and hugging were normal responses to life's ups and downs.

The only door into lightening my mom's mood was humor, and so I teased her: "Tell me how nice I look today. Tell me how much you like my hair." Mom would smile, sometimes chuckle, and either say, "Oh, Linda" or give me the compliment I offered her. No amount of love or playful prodding would change Mom's manera de ser.

I turned my attention toward someone right under my nose, someone who had toiled in Mom's shadow of negativity her whole life. Susan had become my compañera de corazón in the midst of this interminable storm. She was the one I turned to, our lives like parallel tracks of pain and neglected needs.

Hanging up, I gathered my courage and looked at Tot's picture, still silent. Miguel's shadow lived to the right of the cropped photo. I called him. Wishing I could have flown down and given it the importance it truly deserved, I was holding on to Tot with one finger, como una niña, and reaching out to Miguel with the other. He had arrived home from a job site. Like me, he was self-employed and his business came in spurts.

"You are my hermano. Our father never did it right, and I followed him without thinking." I held my breath. He had every right to be furious.

"Pues sí, that's how it was," Miguel answered in a subdued tone.

"I promise things will be different. And I am sorry. I don't know what else to say." I rushed my words to fill the space, pat down the sting of my shame.

All this was in Spanish. While we intermixed languages for the first twenty years of knowing each other, I had moved us permanently to Spanish once my twins were born. It kept us in waters familiar to him, waters that kept me moving.

"Gracias, hermanita. Te quiero mucho."

His verbal and physical cariño had stood out for years. Too much affection before had made me think someone wanted something I didn't want to give up. Not anymore. I had responded with gratitude to his affection over the last few years, especially after Tot's death.

"I love you too, hermano." I choked on my words, grateful for how easy he had made it for me. It was time I remembered I was fifth in line among the siblings, practically the baby at forty.

୬

Imbued with my new commitment, I coaxed everyone to go to Palm Springs after Christmas. My kids saw it as a vacation to see their family. I saw it as a way to change the tide, to have Miguel join our family for an occasion when we normally wouldn't have included him.

The accommodations placed us in a quandary as to where to put Mom and Miguel. Carolyn and I had a room with the kids, Susan and her two sons had another, and she did not want my mother's claws nearby without Fred to shield her.

And what about Miguel? He ended up in his own room for the first night while my mom went with Eddy and Shan-Yee. The next morning, Mom ranted about Shan-Yee taking too much time in the bathroom and insisted on a different room. I sat in my room with Eddy and Shan-Yee, debating options.

We were not ready for this, not in our torn-up states. Susan surviving her second Christmas without Fred; my mom surviving her third without Tot; Susan's sons' disillusionment; me surviving my starved relationship; Carolyn still grieving her mother who had died a year before.

Joy was not flowing except with my cuates, who were getting un helado with Tía Sue, their cousins, and Carolyn.

"Where are we going to put Mom? I can't have her, and Susan won't either. That leaves us with nothing!"

"Relax." Eddy's voice could have been my father's.

"*No!* Don't tell me to relax, as if I am the problem. I am so sick of your attitude." I got up abruptly and walked out of the room. I couldn't stand that word, said to me so many times by Tot with a patronizing tone.

Wandering around the garden two floors down, I found a bench and sat down. After facing my dad's secrets, I couldn't stomach anything that reminded me of his "Tot knows best" attitude. Yes, I did need to relax, but not on command.

Returning to my room an hour later, Susan was there with Carolyn and the kids.

"Mom is going to stay in Miguel's room," Susan said.

I almost laughed, thinking I should stalk out more often. Eddy and I made up the only way we knew how – by ignoring what had happened and pretending to move on.

This trip was one of my more ridiculous ideas unless I imagined the alternative: my mom's home full of the exposed rot of secrets. My first attempt to direct my family's drama had opened to mixed reviews.

15.
Intentional Lies

"MOM IS GONE."

Susan's voice pulled me from the bathroom, where I had been on my knees, my hands splashing in bubbly water with the twins.

"I went by around three, and the car wasn't there. I stopped by while doing errands but she isn't back. I called Gloria and she hadn't heard from her."

"Should I come down?"

"No, let's give it a few more hours. The police are looking for her."

I hung up and released my breath, along with my rising panic. I poured clean water over Gina, pulled her out, and rubbed her wet hair dry.

"Mami's sad," she said. My tears were telling her what I did not.

"Sí, querida. My mami got lost." I held back my sob as I helped her pull her flowered pajama top over her head and then asked Carolyn to put the kids to bed. I grabbed clothes out of my closet and checked flights to LA, a dull headache invading my temples.

After giving my queridos their nigh-nigh besos, I sat at my computer responding to emails. My eyes kept looking at the time.

Susan called at ten-thirty p.m. The police had discovered Mom driving down the wrong side of the street.

She was home sleeping now, having mumbled something about the airport and her luggage. I booked a nine a.m. flight. I should have felt frightened by the image of my mom driving down the wrong side of the street, but my image of her as indomitable overran my fear.

We scheduled an emergency meeting with the Rancho Los Amigos medical staff who had tested her a month before. Gloria stayed with Mom, and Susan and I drove the forty miles to Downey, each in a cocoon of exhaustion. We were ushered into a large room and introduced to two doctors and a social worker. Eddy was on speakerphone.

"She definitely tests as having Alzheimer's," said the doctor closest to me.

This wave crashed on top of me. I did not fight the tumbling, just closed my eyes and waited to be deposited on the shore.

"What does that mean?" Susan asked. Her lips were pressed together, her chin wrinkling as it did when she was close to tears.

"It means she will continue to experience decreased short-term memory," said the social worker. "She may find it hard to plan or finish everyday tasks. What happened yesterday is typical—becoming lost in her own neighborhood, forgetting where she is and how she got there, and not knowing how to get back home."

The social worker passed us several pamphlets of information.

"Last week I came across bills from two different burial services. I cancelled one," Susan said.

I turned to look at my sister. She hadn't told me this, and I hadn't told her about my relationship difficulties. We were protecting each other, bailing out the family boat on opposite sides, hiding problems from each other.

"I suggest getting your name on her bank account so you can check her expenses. Or better yet, give her a specified amount of cash and no checkbook or credit card," said the social worker.

"How do you expect us to do that? She's already suspicious of our motivations, and you're telling us she will probably become even more paranoid as the disease progresses," Susan said.

I looked at their impassive faces and then down at the pamphlet. "'Loss of initiative.' We thought she was depressed," I said.

"It could be both, couldn't it?" Eddy's voice floated out of the speaker.

"Definitely. We recommend a book called *The 36-Hour Day*. Please let us know if anything else comes up," said the social worker.

The staff rose and shook our hands.

"So much for pretending Mom is going to snap out of it. We had better interview potential stealth caregivers who can pose as renters because she can't have her car. Where is it now?"

"It's at my house." Susan said. "I'll set up appointments while you're down here."

A few hours later, I fruitlessly explained to my furious mother for the fifth time why she couldn't have her car. "Mom, you were driving down the *wrong* side of the street."

Her eyes blazed and she hit the kitchen table with the palm of her hand. "¡Mentirosa!"

She was right; I was a liar. I had learned from the best. I got up before yelling or crying and walked outside into her garden, circled the aguacate trees, resting my smooth palms on the rough bark. "Help me with your vieja, Tot."

Pushing the swing that hung from a rope on the verge of unraveling, I surveyed the unpicked fruit littering the grass. When I came back inside and called the social worker, she suggested I get comfortable with intentional lies.

I went to the cocina to get a cup of coffee, held the mild brew in two hands and faced my mom, now sitting calmly reading yesterday's newspaper.

"Mom," I said in a relaxed, low voice, "your car is in the shop. It will be ready tomorrow." I waited for her to bristle.

"Okay. ¿A qué hora lo recogemos?" Her voice had lost its previous fury, as if I had said dinner was ready. It was one of those mood swings from antagonism to calm described in the pamphlet.

"Uh, we can get it around noon."

I stayed another two days to help with "renter" interviews and to pick up prescriptions.

"Vitamins," I whispered to Susan as I hugged my sister goodbye. "Tell her they're vitamins."

❧

It was arrogant to try and save others caught in an undertow when I was drowning right next to them. My relationship was ending with a whimper, a quiet slipping away of the impulse that drove us together. This slow drip of the faucet was staining our lives a dirty copper and driving me to tighten the handle even though I knew the damage could only worsen. We didn't argue, break cookie jars, or vent our spite. I regret that, as it might have allowed us to face our loss together.

I had been looking for answers to my spiritual desolation and had circled back again and again to a despair that did not leave me. Even when I fit nicely into an outside of the box lifestyle it pinched, like the cheap shoes I used to buy at Payless that only gave me blisters.

૨૦

I tiptoed to the bathroom after returning from LA and looked at my face in the mirror, saw the alarm in my eyes, imagined my father's eyes right before death.

Susan had told me, "Be glad you weren't there to see him die. I held his hand and watched him gasp until his lungs stopped breathing."

There was nothing worse than slow suffocation, lungs becoming less and less yours, taken over by a silent, foreboding colonizer raping your cells, sucking the life out of you.

૨૦

My home cradled two children who were smack dab in a sand castle about to be hit by a wave just as they were entering kindergarten. A new school system with families who would make up stories about our two-mom family like I made up stories about Tot's first familia. I had wondered how Tot left his family. I felt the slightest twinge of empathy for how hard that moment might have been for him, even though my departure would be profoundly different.

The first person we keep secrets from is ourselves. What were mine now with my cuates? I was going to leave their mother, and I was not a lesbian.

I didn't tell them the first for almost a year because I couldn't make the words come out. Instead I deluded myself with a scenario of converting the basement into a separate space for me, fantasizing about a family room where the units would converge. I looked for any option other than leaving my queridos or staying in a relationship based on parenting. If Gina got hurt or if Teo had one of his now rare asthma attacks, I wanted to be there to wipe their tears and put a Band-Aid on their rodilla as I sang: "Sana, sana, colita de rana. Si no sanas hoy sanaras mañana." I will wait until I actually move out, I told myself; they are too young to understand, I told myself.

I never directly told them the second secret about my changing identity because I did not have the words even for myself. Being a lesbian had made so much sense intellectually and emotionally. I loved a tribe where my femaleness was the best, most beloved thing about me. I did not want to give up the self-love I had gained, but my relationship was too full of dents from my race and class differences with Carolyn that we could not even articulate well, much less resolve. More importantly, I preferred men as sexual partners and finally admitted it. None of my good friends were surprised when I shared my re-entry into heterosexuality. It was an important awakening towards my path to self-love and community, but did not ultimately resonate with my heart and body.

My son's drawing from a snow trip with another family last winter hung above my desk. I always tended the woodstove fire, and this one had a brick ceiling that kept falling into the fire. Teo's picture showed me rushing to the stove to, once again, carefully maneuver the brick back up to rest precariously on the shelf without getting burned. My decision would not feel loving to my queridos, but I could not give up feeding my inner fire so I could protect them in the long haul. I no longer wanted to code switch in my own home. I no longer wanted to hide in my place of rest. I no longer wanted to translate myself to myself or anyone else. I wanted a home where my children did not have to code switch.

&

Once I told Carolyn our relationship was over—had been over for years—I stopped trying to get along. The pain of how deeply our differences complicated our communication hit me square in the face. I hated unpeeling our onion because we had both tried so hard and had neglected ourselves and each other so much.

We untwined the two-mom routine that had held our lives close for five years. I moved into my back room office. There was actually very little to do, as I already used the closet for my clothes. I consolidated my desk and opened the futon couch to be my bed.

The upcoming Thanksgiving promised to be a painful one with my mom and Carolyn. Both were depressed and bereft, with me no longer thinking I could heal their wounds. I did not mean to cause pain, to seem superior and all knowing. I meant to save and protect my soul and theirs.

A local group had put out a call for essays on mothering, and I squeezed out time to write a short essay a day before the deadline. Not only was it accepted, they decided to name the small book for my story: *The Life I Now Live*. I was tired of leading such a consequence-conscious life. I couldn't turn my back on this gift of writing, nor was I willing to let it squeeze all the whimsy out of my life.

16.
Crazy with a Purpose

JUMPED AT THE CHANCE TO ATTEND A WRITING retreat in Sierra Hot Springs the summer of 2000. Writing called to me as a salve, a private entry into my fierce and weary heart.

I hadn't been alone and unencumbered in awhile; I felt my body breathing deeply as the beauty of the Sierras unfolded on the drive. After arriving and tossing my duffle bag on the floral bedspread, I joined a group of women around the dining room table.

The first exercise was a visualization that involved going deep inside one's body. Turning inward, I saw my body empty, dark, bluish-black. I went into my right leg and the ligament was white with a black, jagged hole. Then it slowly became tinged with green, and it seemed possible to converse with pain as a way to heal it.

The instructor Terry asked us on the morning of the second day: "What is the story that haunts you? That you don't know how to tell, that was passed on to you?"

My gut baulked, but I wrote it down: "Tot's story of growing up, leaving his family, starting another."

While I listed other possibilities, this had the scent my nose wanted to follow. It held decisive truths about my current life—my own wish to grow up and beyond my past and stop the chain reaction of secrets.

When Terry described a story as a record of change, a well of excitement shot through my body and out the pen onto paper.

Arriving home two days later, I resolved to write about my father's life, about the ways we had protected him, holding onto his image as an upright man despite an egregious act. I hired a coach to keep me on track with my writing, but our check-ins were mostly me telling her about the unexpected rapids and swirling eddies that knocked me off my writing plan.

"The kids got sick."

"My mom's caretaker quit."

"My client freaked out and I had to do an unplanned intervention with staff."

The Monday before leaving for our usual Thanksgiving in LA, I called my coach for our weekly session.

"What do you want to commit to for your writing?" she asked.

"I need to meet my Mexican sisters."

"This week?"

"No." I laughed. "But soon. I need to hear their stories so I can write my own."

"That's a big commitment, Linda, in the midst of everything else."

My body pulsed like a giant heartbeat, rebuffing her gentle warning. "It's crazy, but it's crazy with a purpose."

"What would be the first step you can do by next Monday?"

"That's easy! I will talk to Miguel when we go down to LA this week. It will give the despairing landscape a twist of possibility."

Miguel and I were the middle children in each trio, reluctant heroes who had inherited our father's attraction to tilting at windmills. Even though I hadn't yet asked, there was no doubt he would say yes. I was ready for family beliefs to shift and allow the tide of life to flow like never before. Freedom was the flip side of duty, two sides of the same coin. Choosing both meant risking both. Like my parents, I was crossing borders for a better life; the risks were as yet indecipherable.

After perusing my regular writing goals, I knew they were beyond my reach that week. Instead, I penned a poem:

> Mom's rhythm lost is mine found
> her language devalued is mine to honor
> her memories of pain are mine to forgive
> new beginnings bubble up in the maelstrom of
> regret and loss that swirls in my heart
> looking for healthy tissue to nurture, atrophied
> muscles to pump oxygen into
> unabashedly breaking laws about the old dream
> we were handed as our salvation

I then got up from my desk and pulled out my suitcase. As I opened my closet and stood thinking about the LA weather, Teo walked in and hopped onto the futon couch, resting his head on the black-and-white striped pillow, moving his index finger in circles and following it with his eyes.

"Are you daydreaming, querido?" He often would stop in the middle of the day and sit, his eyes seeming to look past whatever was happening to another world.

"Yes."

"What do you think about when you daydream?" I asked, sitting next to his feet and holding them gently.

"I see a cow."

"¿Es negro, moreno o blanco?"

"It's black."

"¿Es un toro o una vaca?"

"A vaca."

"Does it talk to you?"

"No, it's on an island, eating grass."

I smiled, imagining this cow on an island. After that day, we would ask him when he got a faraway look on his face if he was with the vaca on the island. His answer was often "yes."

17.
A Fragile Hope

IN CHILDHOOD, SUSAN AND I HAD LIVED IN OUR own separate worlds, even if my mom dressed us like twins. As young girls, we watched TV and chose different characters as fantasy marriage mates. On *Star Trek*, I chose Captain Kirk *and* the doctor, Bones. Susan chose Spock. She identified with his logical approach, eschewing feelings in favor of what was measurable and provable. We shared the same bedrooms with matching bedspreads for sixteen years but rarely shared our fears.

After I graduated from college and moved back to LA, we cautiously circled closer to our own and each other's corazones. I encouraged her through her first pregnancy, including being present at the home birth, and she supported my decision to join a social justice community on skid row, buoying each other up each time our parents shook their heads in disapproval.

The slight variation in skin tone between us, she a mocha to my café latte, shaped her experiences profoundly. She told me how excited she felt when another brown Latina joined her class in second grade so she wasn't the only one. Not fully comfortable in our home or outside cultures, she chose Latinos and I fled to white people.

By the time Tot died, we were speaking openly of our daily quandaries. Like the mom who now drove us loca with worry, we burrowed into tasks instead of what we needed—a good, long cry—several, in fact. Susan translated her need for care into manicures and pedicures, I with occasional massages and long, hot showers after soccer games. It wasn't nearly enough. She was too skinny, the manchas on my face too dark and pronounced. She couldn't muster any excitement about my trip, more focused on managing mom's "housemate," our provisional solution to her mental and emotional surrender.

In January 2001, I arrived in Los Angeles to give Susan a mini-reprieve from Mom. As I drove Susan home, she casually mentioned she had met our older sisters several years ago, between the time Tot confirmed their existence and his death.

"Point one, I lived here when Rosita came up to visit and shop in the garment district for her business. And point two, I worked for Mexicana Airlines at the time, so I saw them on a few of my business trips. It hit me when I met Tere—'I think she's my sister too. I think they're my sisters.' It was really nice. I met Tere's children briefly and they showed me pictures—it was like a honeymoon when everyone only sees the positive. It felt good." Susan paused. "On the other hand, the honeymoon is over with Frances." Frances was the caregiver who Mom thought was renting a room from her.

"What did she do now?" I asked.

"She called to say Mom yelled at her," said Susan.

"Big deal."

Frances required as much care as Mom, but the thought of searching for another caregiver made us both cringe.

"There's more. She went out to the backyard to calm down and Mom left the house."

"Incredible. Did Frances find her?"

"She was on the phone with me when a car pulled up and Mom got out. She had walked to her bank five blocks away and asked a stranger for a ride home."

"What is the matter with Frances?" I asked.

"I know. Miguel's new girlfriend, Violeta, likes Mom and, more importantly, Mom likes her, so I am thinking of asking if she is interested."

We arrived at Susan's apartment. She rummaged through her desk and pulled out a photo.

"This is Arieti, Tere's daughter. She must be about twenty years old now."

I looked at the school portrait of a lovely brown-haired child of about eight, her resemblance to Gina striking, the sparkling dark eyes, the strong cheekbones and full lips.

She sighed. "Give them saludos de mi and call me when you get back."

I hugged her goodbye and left for the airport.

Miguel and I settled into our seats for the three-and-a-half hour flight to México City. I took out my journal and drew a Mexican family tree, exploring branches that had long been hidden. The circles identifying the females and the squares signaling the males grew on the page as Miguel walked me through our sisters' marriages, their children and grandchildren, his uncle Guillermo's two families, Rosita's divorce and la familia's living arrangements.

"And Tere's son is Toño."

"Toño?" I said. "Short for Antonio, like Eddy's son?"

"Pues sí. We have two nephews with the same name."

We continued with the tree as we crossed the many miles to his birthplace, and I looked for changes in tone or facial expression while asking questions. Miguel grimaced and waved his broad hands in front of his face when he spoke of his uncle Guillermo. There was something underneath his surface anger—the grief of being rejected by the two men who should have taken him under their wing—our father and his uncle.

Miguel, Rosita, and Tere only stayed in touch with their uncle Guillermo's secret second family. Their own experience of being kept in the background contributed to them ignoring Guillermo's legal family, even though Miguel and his sisters *were* the first family chronologically and legally.

"So why go now?" Miguel asked.

"I want to understand how the man who raised me abandoned you, thinking I'd never know because he is gone. But our sisters are not gone."

"Pues así es. They are excited for your visit."

One of Teo's favorite stories over the last year had been that of Mulan, the Chinese girl who, disguised as a man, goes to war in place of her father. The Disney movie had been played many times over the last six months because when Teo loved a movie, we watched it until we knew all the songs. I was like Mulan, doing my father's work. Tot was never able to bring his two families together, but maybe I could.

As Miguel and I walked out of customs, my right eye twitched. Each step toward the frosted glass doors felt like the slow climb up the first hill on a roller coaster as I gripped the safety bar. *Why, oh, why, am I doing this?*

Miguel's familia ran to embrace him affectionately. He was the tawny center of a sunflower, they the golden petals that surrounded him. Standing awkwardly, words from a Sesame Street song came into my head about one thing not belonging here, one thing not being the same.

The outsider designation descended on me like it did on Miguel in Los Angeles. The hugs they gave me were sincere; the smiles welcomed me, but were tinged with caution. It was going to be harder than I could have ever let myself know, like the first time I went to the waves with my father. *Ayúdame, Tot, ayúdame otra vez. Sprinkle your children with angel dust, aními anos to unite the blood that flows in all our veins and pumps our hearts full of longing.*

They asked after Susan and Eddy. Rosita expressed her wish that one day all six of our father's children could be together. I smiled, right there with her in that dream. My new oldest sister was fifty-five, with short blonde hair and dark roots. Her face was as round as mine was narrow and tapered.

Tere, only three and a half years older than me, also showed the remnants of a dye job, the dark orange waves cascading to just below her shoulders. Her face was round also, and smaller than my big cabezota. I wished for some undeniable feature that, if substituted from one body to another, would fit perfectly, corroborating without a doubt we shared the same father, but it wasn't there.

Victor, Tere's husband of twenty-three years, motioned us to follow him to the garage. His dark eyes had met mine with a mix of candor and curiosity. He stayed close to Tere the whole time, guiding her with his hand and watching her with a protective gaze. We wove through the clamor that is Benito Juárez International Airport and I felt joy at hearing Spanish surround me. We squeezed into two cars after Victor arranged our luggage in the trunk, his sturdy frame bristling with energy.

I slid into the back seat between Arieti, Tere's daughter and Joanna, Rosita's daughter. My nieces easily called me tía, and that little word was like the soft kisses I had given my six-year-old twins before I left. I rested between their positive energetic field as the Spanish flowed fast for a few minutes, while Victor directed the car through the garage and turned out into the vast metropolis of el D.F.

"Now I practice English!" Arieti smiled, her dark brown hair pulled back in a clip, a contrast to her peach skin.

"Yes!" Joanna replied. She had a darker olive tone and a short sporty coif.

"No, no, no!" I insisted. "¡Quiero hablar español!"

"You can each speak the other language," Tere responded in her lilting voice. As we drove to Rosita's house, where I would spend the night, Tere pointed out the University where she had worked many years as a professor of business administration, having also received a Masters in Merchandise.

It was late and we agreed to get a good night's sleep. We would meet the following day to visit Chapultepec Park. Tere had also pointed that out on our drive, a vast dark expanse in the middle of the labyrinth of car lights, fast moving cars, and drivers not afraid to honk their horns. Even with the time change that meant it was eight p.m. rather than ten p.m., I collapsed into Rosita's bed, feeling bad that she insisted on staying in the den, then fell into a weary sleep.

In the morning, my stomach grumbled. Knowing their schedule might mean I didn't eat a meal until close to noon, I looked through her cupboard, which were mostly bare, but did find a box of crackers. I wandered into the living room. Her apartment was full of the heavy furniture I equated with middle-class Mexican homes—solid and ornate, European in style. I sat gingerly on the cream-colored couch next to a large glass vase of life-like lilies. I wished I had asked Susan to come with me.

About ten o'clock Rosita descended the spiral metal staircase, her short robe displaying firm, full legs and red toenails. Speaking about our father with cariño, she lit a cigarette and recounted her numerous trips to Los Angeles. She had had a clothing store and flew to LA to shop downtown for women's clothes every three to four weeks for three years. She had even brought her three kids up a few times to meet their abuelo. Rosita had then turned her attention to a cookbook and her trips stopped. Miguel had told me on the plane that Rosita had been separated from her husband for twenty years and still received significant financial support from him. She had a novio, perhaps ten years younger than her, whom I had not yet met.

Rosita lit another cigarette. "I spoke with nuestro papá three days before he died."

It was the same day I spoke with him as I had created my altar.

"I felt the pérdida," she said. "But I was too sick to go to the funeral."

This loss was profound, including much more than the death of her distant father. She dabbed at her eyes. My mind wandered back to the funeral. What would have happened if Rosita, the first-born, had exerted her right to bury her father? We would not have been able to continue with the script, the one that kept her and Tere hidden like I used to hide my stained underwear, an embarrassment I didn't know what to do with.

The phone rang and Rosita spoke briefly with Tere, with whom Miguel was staying. After hanging up, we did not return to the intimacy of our charla and instead climbed the stairs to shower and change. When we reached the top, she turned to me. "Era un lobo."

I nodded. Even though the depiction of wolves as loners was inaccurate, her description of our father as a loner was true for us. He traveled across the border and kept any indecision or pain inside himself, his actions rarely explained. His children were now left as the older generation to decide which of his footprints they wanted to step in and which they would sidestep.

Around eleven, Joanna chauffeured us to Chapultepec Park for a celebratory lunch as it was Miguel's fifty-first birthday. We had the restaurant almost to ourselves. While the day was overcast, the curved glass walls of the restaurant created a light feel to our initial meal together. Ducks and geese floated by in the lake outside.

Tere told me she knew a lot about "tu cultura," placing me in the gringa box. It was true that I was born in the United States, but gringa to me meant someone who had blond hair, a bad accent, and valued Latin America for exotic adventures and cheap purchases. Tere reminded me of Susan in that they were both enamored of facts, especially when their feelings heated up and control was fast desapareciendo. She spouted statistics that glided right past my heart. What struck me was her rage and grief. I knew that undertone like the back of my hand.

Her Spanish became higher and sharper. "The Americans think they can come and do whatever they want. But they forget we are the descendants of nobility. The Aztecs who survived longest and whose blood is in us were those who were the fiercest, the wisest, the proudest."

All I could do was nod, wondering if I would ever be enough to garner Tere's full acceptance. I liked her. She did not make nice, a quality I appreciated even if it sometimes drew blood. I was invading their hard-earned sense of familia, slowly recovered after my father left them for good. Miguel must have been feeding them information for years about me. I was colliding with the stories they had heard about me for thirty years, even longer for Rosita who had met us briefly as children.

The waiter arrived just then with a candle in Miguel's dessert and graciously took our picture. Miguel, a big grin on his face, was surrounded by his hermanas and sobrina, our hands resting on his red and black Nike sweat suit jacket. To the few other diners, I imagine we looked as if we had been together our whole lives. The small glazed vase on the white tablecloth held five bright yellow daisies, one for each of us. It settled me momentarily, this touch of serendipity.

As we waited outside for Joanna to get the car, Tere looked closely at my face. I wondered if she was looking for a resemblance between us.

"We have a good cream in México that is better than whatever you are using for the manchas on your cheeks and forehead," she said. "There was a time when I had really dark ones that looked like a butterfly spread out across my two cheeks. And now look, my skin is clear."

I could see I would get all kinds of consejos from her on this trip. Like mi niña Gina had, Tere had zeroed in on the signs of stress darkening my forehead and cheeks.

Attempting to take a short nap when we returned, I was too anxious to do much other than move from one position to another on Rosita's bed. When I heard the doorbell, I wrapped a shawl around myself and descended the curved staircase. I was met with the smiling faces and abrazos of Arieti and Victor, who joined us for a supper of chicken, salad, rice, and beans that Rosita had ordered from a local woman who often cooked for her.

A few drinks loosened my siblings' tongues. I already knew Miguel and I were lightweights, but it seemed to be a family trait. No one in my genetic family drank much. My parents had a very elaborate bar on wheels with an ancient globe that opened to reveal glasses that were always coated with a film from lack of use. The bottles below were equally dusty.

After dinner, we settled into the living room couch and large armchairs. Miguel's brow wrinkled and he rested his large hands on the edge of a sofa, telling me how his mother worked for thirty years in a tortillera from four a.m. to four p.m., making masa, standing the whole time. Their abuelos had a successful business with molinas that made the masa, and tortilleras that created the finished products sold throughout the city. Teresita's decision to not go with my father wasn't because she'd had the standing her brother Guillermo had in the business or because she was given financial support by her parents. This surprise wave of information erased the lie written on the sand of my mind that her parents had coddled her.

"That's because your querido padre left her," Tere said.

I gazed up, but she was looking at Miguel.

"She was too tired to give us much attention when she was home," Miguel said, shaking his head.

"She never saw anyone else?" I asked.

"No," said Rosita, her throaty voice cutting through the smoke of the one cigarette the family allowed her when they were present.

"When our father left for good," continued Miguel, his speech slower, "my mother's parents came, saying they needed to raise the girls and I needed to take care of my mother."

"For good?"

"Yes," Rosita replied. "Nuestro papá had begun going to the states several years before he left and never came back. I was nine and Tere was one."

"How old were you?" I asked Miguel.

"I was five." His face crumpled and tears streamed down the ruddy cheeks that showed the effects of working in the sun and grit of his demolition business.

Tears rolled down my face and Rosita and Tere were both sniffling. They had lost their mother as well when Tot left.

Miguel leaned forward, his squat fingers interlaced, his forearms resting on his knees. "In my early teens, I was sent to work with my tío Guillermo and supervised one hundred workers at the molino, where they ground the corn for tortillas. Can you imagine me doing that at that age?"

I shook my head. I couldn't imagine any of this without wanting to rage at my father. It stirred a memory—someone telling me my father had worked at a molina for his in-laws, my siblings' abuelos. "And then?"

"Then they sent me to a military school," Miguel said. The all powerful *they* seemed to be the abuelos, taking over once Tot had left them.

Tere looked at me. "Would it have been better if we had told a different story?"

"I didn't come to hear more lies. I came to understand my—our—father's secrets."

Their words pushed over another cart full of sweet connections I had shared with my father over the last ten years before he died, laying waste to my birth and my childhood losses. My mother worked, but she did not work ten-hour days, did not have a brother who pushed her around and kept the best for himself. Any punishment she felt was mostly self-inflicted as she slowly got to know the man she had picked, the man she chose to stay with again and again as his secrets revealed themselves. The man who did not marry her until their firstborn was four months old and never told her that he was a married man.

"When *your* father died I felt nothing," Tere responded. "My abuelo was my father. He was the one who raised me."

Unlike Rosita and Miguel, Tere had not pursued Tot's love and acceptance. We had fallen back, one by one, into our seat cushions. Victor, Joanna, and Arieti had been silent witnesses to this tightly knotted group of siblings. Tere's husband Victor's silence was the most surprising as he had not hesitated to speak up before this conversation. He did look at his watch and quietly tell us it was midnight. We gave the goodnight abrazos and besos that I cherished. The cumbersomeness of the tangle we were loosening lay between us, so much still to be unraveled.

After writing in my journal, I tucked myself into Rosita's flowered sábanas. As I slowly entered sleep, I could almost hear my father's voice. It pleaded for me to imagine him in México, a poor man who married the young daughter of a man of some stature, believing he could prove his mettle. But she adored her father and her brother Guillermo, and everyday they let Tot know he was not good enough for her. He was working ten-hour days, making babies, straining at the bit in his mouth. When his friend Arturo invited him to go to el norte, he went. At first, he believed his wife would join him across the border with their growing family, but she was traditional and refused to leave. His pride compelled him to act decisively, thinking it was his only chance to live his own life.

But at what cost? I wanted to yell. You knew how badly your wife's brother Guillermo behaved toward you. You had to see how he treated others with disregard, driven by greed. You probably knew about his secret second family. Yet you convinced yourself that your young family would be safe without you, that Teresita's parents would step in, would not punish her for choosing you. You forgot the way women and children in your family had forgiven the men at too high a cost.

I slept in with the rest of the household, my nighttime dream still simmering. The anxiety evoked by the dream began boiling and made me want to pack up and go home. I've met them, I've started the journey, I've touched my fears and theirs. No one else had ever ventured into these lies and I now knew why.

As I showered, I cried into the hot water, my body shaking inside the dimly lit stall. I missed my babies. This was the longest I had been away from them. I wanted to see their faces and feel their uncomplicated cariño. As I toweled off, I reminded myself that this was for them, so their welcome would be less clouded with the past. I reached into my purse and fingered their first ever school pictures. I wanted to know how my dad felt when he left his infant daughter, his trusting Rosita, and his little brave son. This question hit me too close to my own split-hearted home. I brushed it away so I could think about day three.

My goals were simple. Parcel out the gifts I'd brought from Susan, don't get too hungry since their meals were less predictable than mine, and visit Frida Kahlo's house. My querida niece Joanna drove Rosita, Tere, and me to the historic Blue House. Rosita looked at Frida's paintings and rolled her eyes. Tere was more conciliatory, acknowledging, "Frida suffered a lot."

My hermanas wandered quickly through the rooms and waited in the colorful patio while I browsed the gift shop. Looking at her more graphic, bloody paintings on key chains and magnets dipped me into the grim images of my siblings' childhood. I left without any purchases.

As we drove home, my goal to not get too hungry was foiled. We drove around for several hours with my sisters and Joanna discussing plans for the next two days and then changing them in between a stop for gas and another stop to pay the phone bill. Joanna described the universities as we passed them.

"That is the Nahuatl College for los ricos." The college named after the original language of the Aztecs catered to the modern day "royalty." Joanna described the Tech College as one where the students studied day and night and relaxed by playing chess with life-size pieces.

That evening, we again gathered at Rosita's home, this time with almost all the grown children. I met Rosita's two sons, Juan José and Juan Carlos, and gratefully hugged my nieces Joanna and Arieti. My siblings' tío Guillermo was not there, but his second family came. The mom Isaura was a short, very serious, religious woman. Two of her children, my siblings' cousins, greeted me with besos. It was funny to hear Miguel's relatives call him "Mike."

Rosita, who did not cook much, had again paid the local woman to bring comida preparada. The feast was served in traditional earthenware full of rice, beans, and carne asada placed on a plastic tablecloth covered with bright red flowers. We sat on the upholstered, plastic covered chairs pushed against the wall. Near the end of the gathering, their cousin Jaime asked me if I had known about my father's Mexican family. His eyes darted around and he rubbed his hands together, admitting how hard it was for him to be a member of the family with no rights and no acknowledgment from Guillermo.

"I can see why you are close," I responded, "especially since your father Guillermo was as neglectful of you as he was of Miguel and my sisters. It's hard to carry that pain."

Tere admitted that her two children didn't know about our father having two families—my visit had forced her to tell them. I wondered whether Tere had kept the whole story from them as had been done to us, each person diluting or deleting facts to protect themselves and others. Tere's voice rose sharply as she told the story of first meeting Tot.

"I was eighteen when I came to Los Angeles." Her voice broke and tears shone in her eyes. "Miguel went to hug tu papá, who put out his arm to stop him, his own son. I saw the hurt in my brother's face and that's when I rejected him as my father."

I had thought Miguel had come alone. I had thought Tere had never considered my dad to be her dad. She must have had some wish to connect with Tot or she wouldn't have had to reject him. That made the scene she recounted even more heart-wrenching.

"Ay, Mami," said Arieti, stroking her mother's hair gently.

As Arieti continued to comfort Tere, I went to the bathroom, closed the door, lowered the lid on the toilet, and sat down. Bowing my head, I reached back with my hands and dug my fingers into my rock-hard shoulder muscles. I needed to hear it all before we could carve a different path. Extricating ourselves from this morass meant ripping open all the floorboards and airing out the dank secrets of almost fifty years. Washing and drying my hands slowly, I returned and sat down next to Tere, leaning into the family circle. Arieti was still stroking her mother's hair, una dulzura my mom would never have allowed from me or anyone else. I felt myself pulling away and pressed my feet into Rosita's crème shag rug.

"What about your last name, Miguel? Why is it Durand?" I asked my brother.

"It's my mother's family name. Our father's last name was Manrique. When mi papá told me to change my first name, I also dropped his family name."

González was yet another sign of betrayal, of a father deleting his past by dropping his father's name and keeping his mother's. My last name should have been Manrique.

"Enough of the sad stories. What should we do on your last day?" Tere's voice was soft and sweet.

Even though it was a night full of tears and rage, I clung to her tender tone so I could stay in one piece, hold on to my last ounce of courage. We agreed to drive to Teotihuacan and visit the pirámides. I fell into the goodbye besos, grateful that no matter how rugged the terrain of the day, this is how we ended. Arieti gave me a long hug, expressing her regret she had to work and could not accompany us. Victor would also not come, as his job as a civil engineer required his presence on weekdays.

Alone in my room, I wrote down stories to share with Susan. Turning back to the family tree, I added the three children of Rosita's oldest son Juan José and corrected a few ages. I then went to the top and added an empty square for my father's papá and a circle for his mamá. Inside her circle I wrote "Concepción González." Inside my abuelo's square I wrote "¿? Manrique."

After a restless night, another pleasant and inviting morning welcomed me. An hour drive took us away from the congestion of the city and into the open savannah that used to be a series of lakes surrounded by the southern stretch of the Sierra Nevada ranges. After parking, Tere, Joanna, and I climbed up to the top of the Templo del Sol. The many steep steps and the Mexican altitude sucked the air out of my lungs. Rosita rested down below, and we waved at each other from across the distance, the mild breeze rustling our hair and cooling us down from the climb. A measure of happiness materialized as I stood atop such a dramatic precipice, the blood and sacrifice of our ancestors binding us together after too many years of unspoken stories and memories.

As we walked along the Street of the Dead to the Pirámide de la Luna, Tere was in her glory, the yellow flowers on her outfit blossoming like the facts she shared as la profesora. She described the tunnel-like cave, ending in a cloverleaf-shaped set of chambers, below the Pirámide del Sol. This cave may have been a "place of emergence," the "womb" from which the first humans came into the world.

It felt rejuvenating to be among our ancestors' great feat and our personal feat of being together after so many years of separation. The sun broke through the cloud cover and we shed our jackets at times, enjoying the warmth on our bare arms. Joanna had been our chauffeur for most of our day trips. Her lively smile softened any remaining pain from our necessary conversations of the nights before. When I locked arms with my hermanas and my niece Joanna, a kind stranger snapped a picture.

Walking back to the car, I pointed to some lettering on a sign. "Look! It's almost Teotli's name!" My son's name was Nahuatl, and here we were in a sacred place of energy.

We met Victor and Arieti at a corner stand for dinner around seven, enjoying birria and sharing stories about the day.

"We passed a pharmacy and Linda bought Eldoquin for her manchas." Tere was delighted to share this bit of news.

I showed them my compras for my kids—an embroidered vest for Teo and a dress for Gina. When I pulled out pictures of my kids, they agreed the resemblance to Tere's kids at that age was striking. I promised to bring them on my next trip.

"And you can see how my manchas are doing!" I pushed Tere playfully with my hand and she laughed loudly.

The next morning came too soon. We entered the hustle of the airport, caught in the surge of people and jumble of emotions airports create. After checking in, we sat in the café near my gate and drank a final cafecito together. Arieti commented on my last name, González, thinking it strange that Americanos use their maternal family's name.

"I think mi papá dropped Manrique in an attempt to cover his tracks. So his niños couldn't find him," I said. Reaching out, I put my hand on hers. "I am glad his plan didn't work."

Soon my flight was announced. I gathered my backpack and started toward the gate. Arieti handed me a piece of paper. We hugged and then I turned to hug my hermanas, flooded with the grief of what we had missed, of the wounds still tender to the touch. Of those yet unexposed, because trust takes time and courage. I couldn't speak, only looked at them each with a glimmer of joy in my eyes that found the same in theirs. I hugged Miguel, who was staying for another week, and whispered, "Gracias."

On the plane, I fished around in my backpack for my journal and tissue as tears came. Poco a poco I told myself. I was glad the next generation wouldn't carry our secrets. My fingers touched the squares and circles that were real people now. There were my three nephews who I met briefly and the two nieces who had welcomed me from the beginning. Manrique was my shadow name, the name that carried my father's secret. I took out my pencil and began adding the circles and squares of my family in the US. I fingered the little square and circle that signified my chiquitos. They had lines that connected them to Carolyn and me. Would they forgive me for the two lines that crossed out my relationship to Carolyn? At times I had felt Teo's anger, his protectiveness toward Carolyn while Gina stayed quiet. I wanted my children's forgiveness for pursuing my dreams, for changing our familia in the hopes of finding one I had no name for yet.

I opened Arieti's card and took in her attempt to write in English:

> Antie,
>
> *I hope you've been as happy as I was with you here. I want to thank you for your love and tenderness to us. We want you to know how much we love you and miss you. I want you to leave*

with a big smile and with many wishes to come back. Please send our love to the family there and tell them that we are specting them and above all this thank you for your help.

I hope the love grows fast and lasts forever. Remember to tell Teo and Gina how much we love them.

Arieti

That was a promise I could keep. Closing my eyes, I sat in a fragile hope that enveloped me like a silk rebozo so fine it could slide through a wedding band.

18.
Puzzle Pieces of Familia

AFTER KINDERGARTEN DREW TO A CLOSE, WE told our almost six-year-old queridos that I would be moving to an apartment two blocks away. Their initial reactions surprised us. Teo asked if he would get a dad and Gina ran to the kitchen to call one of my best friends to tell her. After that, they did not ask many questions, and we focused on helping them enjoy their summer.

I lessened my work schedule to spend more time with them and soak in their energy, but the heaviness of my losses too often felt like wearing a wool sweater on a balmy summer day. When I drove the kids down to LA to celebrate Rafael's graduation from high school, I stopped more frequently to let them run around, stretch my tired legs, and feel the cost of being alone.

Susan had asked us to create a page to give Rafael for a book of wisdom, and mine carried one of Tot's dichos, even as I still processed my sense of betrayal.

> *Since abuelo isn't here to share his wisdom for your journey, I will share in his memory:*
> *He would have said: "There are no problems, there are only situations."*
> *I never understood what he meant and I certainly never asked him to explain! What I understand now is that when I think of*

something as a problem, I tend to have a nega-
tive attitude about it and I worry that I can't
find a solution. When I think of it as a situation,
I have a more positive attitude and I believe that
a solution is possible.

My attitude about Tot was on the negative side of the scale, but I remained positive about my newfound relationship with my Mexican family, especially when my fingers touched Arieti's note on my desk.

As I observed Fred put his arm around Susan, I was grateful we were unofficially celebrating their reconciliation. His added energy and big heart lightened the daily grind, especially for Susan. She had gained weight in the last few months and I inherited her "skinny" grief clothes. Fred and I shared a tearful hug, as we had when he left two and a half years before. My sister might have wanted to marry Spock as a young girl, but Fred was the antithesis of distant and unemotional. The two of us, along with Miguel, surrounded her again with our exuberant aquarian decibels.

"Did you get my email about dates for Mom to come up?" I asked as I loaded the last of our bags into the Jetta.

"Yes. Eddy is coming down in July and I'll send Mom up in early August so she can be there for your kids' sixth birthday."

"Wish you'd come. You know how much the kids want you at their party."

"I know, but we need a break."

We hugged and I settled in for the five-and-a-half-hour drive to Berkeley. Paying heed to two sets of needs with one pair of hands and an exhausted spirit had delayed my departure from what had been my kids' home since birth.

Traveling alone made me ask Carolyn to come with the kids and me to México in July. This, our last "family" trip, was a visit to my familia en México—a crazy with a purpose plan to have my dissolving family rub shoulders with my fledgling Mexican one. Even though I arrived a few days earlier to prepare the way, I kept my mouth shut about my break-up, simply saying their other mom was bringing them and offering no other datos. No questions were asked.

When Tere, Arieti, and I arrived at the airport to pick up Carolyn and the kids, they weren't at the regular exit. I paced for half an hour, the sweat running down my arms and my heart pressing against my ribs. The message board said they had arrived an hour earlier, plenty of time to pass through immigration and be running into my anxious arms. I ran, dodging pile after pile of families and leaving Tere and Arieti behind.

After one last turn, I spotted my queridos standing with Carolyn.

"I was so worried." My voice was ragged as I grabbed my chamacos, who were nonplussed and wiggled out of my tight abrazo. Grabbing their hands, I escorted them down the hallway, Carolyn trailing behind us. We met Tere and Arieti almost immediately.

"Te presento a Gina y Teo y Carolyn." I stood awkwardly in the discomfited pieces of my life as Tere and Arieti gave my kids and Carolyn hugs. As my children nodded in comprehension of their second idioma, gratitude sweetened the bitterness of my soon to be two-household family.

We arrived at Tere and Victor's home in a colonia located about an hour and a half south of the heart of México City. Dusk was settling on us as we pulled into their carport. We each grabbed a suitcase while Arieti pulled the heavy sliding metal door shut and locked it. Tere opened the door into her casa as their perrita Gijo ran to greet us. Gina and Teo dropped their backpacks and kneeled down to pet her soft fuzzy body. The light was dim as we made our way into their small living room, part of the downstairs that was one room with a large sofa, matching armchair, big screen TV, and small coffee table. The other half of the room was the dining area.

Tere offered us juice and we sat around the oblong dining room table. The glass top covered a lace tablecloth that brushed against my knees as I sat down. I could see Tere speaking to the maid in the small kitchen, reviewing the chores she had finished and discussing the laundry and ironing needed for the next day. Looking up, I saw a posed picture of Arieti from the shoulders up with her joyful smile and a bouquet.

"Tu quinceañera?" I asked and she nodded. It was mounted next to a dark wood china cabinet full of glassware. To the right was a wall of windows. Dark outlines of small trees and bushes lined the high concrete walls encasing a small grass area.

After a light meal of a sopa, rice, and fruit, Tere directed us up the metal, spiral stairs to the second floor. Family photos lined the walls, including her wedding pictures. There were three small bedrooms and she motioned us into the master bedroom, which was dominated by a king-size bed.

"Where will you sleep?" I said.

"Don't worry," Tere replied. "I will sleep in Arieti's room and Victor will sleep on the couch. It is only one night as we are going to Acapulco tomorrow."

I hadn't been in the same bed with Carolyn for a year. As I read a nighttime story, the kids snuggled in the middle of the bed as a buffer between their moms when we eventually came to bed. I noticed a large, framed photograph of a woman on the wall. I had a feeling she was my father's first wife; that would not bring me the sweet dreams I sang about to Teo and Gina.

"Buenas noches, queridos."

When I walked down the stairs, Carolyn was speaking her elementary Spanish to Tere at the dinner table. I almost chuckled as I sat down, wondering why the people in my life kept agreeing to my often ill-conceived trips. Tere reviewed our plan to leave in the morning for Acapulco. Her daughter Arieti would drive us while her husband Victor, Rosita, and she took a second car.

"We'll find a hotel right on the beach where there isn't any trash," said Tere.

"Trash? Is it that bad?" I asked.

I was bone-tired, but even though the kids would be sleeping between us, I would rather explore the level of basura en la playa than go lay down. In fact, I would rather find out who the woman in the picture was, so I asked.

"Mi mamá," said Tere. I didn't know then she meant her abuela, not her biological mother, forgetting she saw her abuelos as her parents. After an hour we gave the good night besos I loved, and I closed the bedroom door with a measure of dread.

Once we were checked into the Acapulco hotel, I changed into my bathing suit and walked to the beach with the kids, settling into the soft sand with Rosita. I eyed my sister, the one I had first met like a flash of light thirty years ago while I hid with Susan in my room, erasing her like the waves had smoothed out our footprints so only the tiniest trace remained. Rosita's ringed fingers sifted through sand that was a few tones darker than her pink skin.

"I was only nine when my Papi left, Linda." Her light brown eyes looked out across the protected cove to a small island perhaps a mile out. "I was so heartbroken."

"And Tere hates him because she has no good memories like you," I said.

Rosita and Miguel had an optimism that reached a higher octave than the rest of us. Snuggling down into my sand nest, a soft breeze lifted my shoulder length curls and flew them like the colorful papalotes at the far end of the beach.

"What was it like for you to know we existed?" Rosita asked.

I looked toward the three round towers of a five-star hotel, unable to meet her eyes. "I didn't think about it, and Miguel never said anything to me in the years he lived near us. And my—*our* dad said nothing until Susan asked him directly about you nine years ago."

"Look. Se ve bonita." She smiled and pointed to Gina, perched on a plastic chair about fifteen feet from us under a white umbrella, her thin, strong legs dangling. The señora's fingers expertly braided a long strand of her hair. Gina saw us and carefully waved her right hand, a shy grin on her face.

My abuela's craggy dark skin matched that of the señora tying off Gina's final braid with a tiny rubber band, although my abuela rarely smiled in our home like this señora.

"Were you in touch with our abuela?" I asked.

"Not too much, although I did see my tía for many years." Rosita shifted her body.

"Tía? You mean our dad had a sister? I thought he was an only child. Do you know where she is now?" I asked.

"No, I lost touch after I got married. I can't even remember her name."

Why does one forget a tía's name? I ran my upper teeth back and forth on my lower lip and considered the possibility of an aunt somewhere in México. I might even have cousins that had no idea we existed. Stretching my legs out, the small waves no longer lapped at my toes as the tide pulled away from us. I looked toward the umbrellas where Carolyn sat building a sandcastle with Teo. Tere rested in a chair nearby, her eyes closed.

"How long have you been with Carolyn?" Rosita asked.

"We're not together anymore."

I didn't mention my eleven years of lesbian identity collapsing; my own lies like spilt leche I was still mopping up.

Gina ran towards her newly found tía and me. "I'm hungry, Mami." She flopped into my lap.

I wrapped my arms around her wriggly limbs, her legs a smaller, more slender replica of my own. I had no doubt they would one day dwarf mine. Her braids were silky smooth as I rubbed my fingers down them. "Vámonos," I said, motioning toward the others with my chin.

As we walked together, holding hands, a small boy approached us, offering chicle in little boxes for us to buy. My father could have been one of these boys growing up, selling whatever he could to make ends meet with his mother. Perhaps he decided early that life was not fair and that no one could save him but himself.

After a seafood buffet at the hotel, we hustled to the cars and drove to La Quebrada. We arrived in time for the first of the four evening shows, where divers plunge one hundred and thirty-six feet into a ten- foot crevice full of aquamarine swells. The two divers perched like statues across from us, carrying torches to illuminate their graceful falls.

I leaned into the rocky gap to inhale the ocean air and gather the ganas to reassemble the puzzle pieces of my familias. To my left, Carolyn stood with our twins, pulling on their chamarras against the cool twilight breeze. To my right stood Tere and Rosita. Like the divers, we were taking a leap of faith that demanded patience and bravery. I reached into the waters of my memory to the first time I had rested my arms on this cement ledge.

When I was eight years old, my family crossed the Tijuana border for a summer vacation. We traveled down the Autopista del Sol Highway from México City to Acapulco in a 1957 Chevrolet Kingswood station wagon, our belongings strapped down on the roof. We three kids slept in the back with the seat folded down and sheets shielding us from the ninety-degree heat.

We didn't visit any family; I thought of us as tourists. I followed Tot and my mom to these ledges and my small arms, like those of my twins, felt the rough stone and marveled at the diver who bent his legs and launched out into the fluid arms del cielo, although we had come in the daylight. My father's hands rested lightly on my shoulders and his eyes followed the divers as mine did, our chins lowering down to our necks as our mouths stretched into delighted grins. He was not muy cariñoso, so both contentment and discomfort sloshed in my stomach.

"Wow, Tot, that was great!"

I uttered a rare compliment about his patria in English, smiling. I was mostly mute in public during our trips south, because I felt uncomfortable speaking Spanish. He and my mom avoided the rough edges of English once they hit the black asphalt of México.

After the diving session ended, we climbed up the broad stone steps to our car and I settled in the back seat between Susan and Eddy. The Las Brisas hotel where we were staying was only ten minutes away. I planned to slide into my damp, red polka dot bathing suit and head back to the gentle waves.

"You wanna go with me?"

Susan and Eddy nodded. Pleased with their promise, I reached down to the floor of the car and picked up my Nancy Drew mystery.

☙

"Linda?" Tere's voice brought me back, thirty-one years after my last visit. "Have you been here before?"

I looked at her, noting the green contacts she wore that shone in the dusk. When I came to La Quebrada the first time, Tere would have been around twelve years old and had been living with her abuelos for eleven years. She would have been looking into the tunnel labeled adolescence, feeling vulnerable and curious.

"Sí, many years ago."

Many years and many secrets later. I had one more secret to add to our overflowing bucket. A tía, maybe a whole other branch of familia out there. By the time we reached the hotel and kissed goodnight, my stomach was cramping and I raced to the bathroom. I promptly fell asleep in the double bed I shared with Teo.

Two more days of sun and beach passed with me eating yogurt and toast, but with no change in my stomach's ability to digest my food.

"Go to the hotel's medical clinic," Tere urged me again and again.

I was adamant in refusing until the third day, my distrust of western medicine giving way to my wish to eat one of the delicious meals I kept watching everyone else eat. She accompanied me to the infirmary, where a doctor gave me a shot and pills. By mid-afternoon my body was back in business and I rued my stubborn insistence on toughing it out, especially because it was our last day.

As we loaded up our equipaje in the two cars, Arieti asked her mom if she would drive back, as she was feeling tired.

"I can." My words surprised everyone. I missed driving and the road had been so smooth and easy on the way here. Driving also made me feel in control and this trip was full of what my writing group called "unexploded emotional bombs."

They paused and pondered the notion of letting the "gringa" tía drive. "Claro que sí!" Victor gave his approval and we were off.

The kids and Carolyn piled into the back seat and Arieti slid into the front seat. As we passed the first tollbooth, the day faded into a penumbra. I steered the car through curves that eventually blended into the dark landscape. A few raindrops turned into hammering rain. The wipers hardly kept up. I leaned forward, squinting at the road and the blurred taillights of Victor's car, my beacon in this downpour.

The kids were asleep, having folded themselves into

sweet cinnamon rolls, their heads sharing Carolyn's lap. The rain subsided by the time we reached the outskirts of México City almost four hours later. I pulled into their driveway, tired but pleased.

"Let's go buy some Negro Modelo—I'll make you a michelada." Victor laughed. "You are a bonafide driver. That rain was una tormenta!"

We walked a block down to a store and returned to the kitchen where he squeezed several limes into each glass and then poured the malty beer in.

"Salud." We touched glasses and I savored the cool, tart taste and this calm between storms.

"Let's play Continental!" I said.

Arieti was already at the dining room table expertly shuffling two decks together. Carolyn and I had become addicted in Acapulco, competitive souls that we were. The game, which Carolyn likened to gin rummy, had fifteen different rounds that required players to create different combinations of threes and straights. For each new round, there was a different wild card and an additional card was dealt.

"Oh, no," Rosita moaned on one of the rounds when only one person got to put their cards down and the rest of us accumulated mega-points.

Arieti grinned as she added up all our negative points. She was often the winner in these two to three hour games.

"I was so close!" I groaned, staring at the many cards in my hand. "Just one more time around."

"The nine is the wild card, three sets of threes and one straight. Deal to us thirteen cards," said Arieti, practicing her English.

The faces around the table exhibited various shades of concentration. We fanned the many cards out in our left hands and organized them with our right, pulling and placing cards carefully so as to not disturb the delicate balance.

Returning to México was pure instinct, pure animal knowledge. Sleeping in Tere and Victor's bed again with the matriarch hovering above and Carolyn two children away from me stripped me down to the studs of my foundation. While it made no sense for me to have invited Carolyn, I did it for those two sleeping bodies between us—to make sure someone besides me would put their needs first. I sensed the massive work required when I returned, leaving my home of ten years, my children, and one more illusion of family bliss.

Interlude

WHAT IS IT ABOUT THE DIVERS AT LA QUEBRADA that draws me in—the sight of a small statuesque man on a rock high above the turquoise Acapulco waters? Looking down solemnly, he knows that curious and doubtful eyes are watching with breath held tight, as if I am the one about to plunge down into the water, sometimes alone, sometimes with other divers, sometimes daring a somersault at fifty-five miles an hour. What thoughts go through his head as he raises his hands and salutes the crevice below? There has never been a professional fatality since they began diving, but still, he could be the first to shatter his body against the rocks. What then? What happens to these men over the years, what happens in their homes, what happens to their souls?

He is a symbol to me, one who risks his life to feel the rush of air and the snap of water breaking as he disappears into los brazos del mar. There is no turning back once his feet spring up and away from the cliff edge worn smooth from innumerable soles. He has worked his way there—starting as a child—leaning on the ledge where I now lean. Deciding one day he will climb the rocks, feel the steps hewn from other brown feet clamoring up like mountain goats, deft and determined, but also desperate to reach the top.

I, like the divers, am captivated by vistas, by large expanses of brilliant blues and acrid salt, gulls screeching and savoring their fresh fish flesh; I know his journey.

From the waters that gently cradle him before his first climb, lapping at his ears as he ponders why he will risk the life he knows. The first dive is from only a few feet up, the ease of it soothing the abject terror of his shaking muscles. When he surfaces, he is determined to swim to the familiar shore, but finds his bare feet kicking him towards the rocks again and again, pretending it will be his last dive when his legs or alma wobbles. He persists, pushing forward each time fear grips his ankles and won't let him go, especially if he misjudges his trajectory and the ocean pummels his head as if he has hit cement.

He is watched, judged, coached, cajoled. Unrelentingly, mercilessly, repeatedly. He cannot fail, cannot stop the climb, cannot swim away from his destino, his don, and his compadres.

The scrapes mount, the ache sinks into his bones, and the small steps pull him higher and further from the waves and the cries of those he loves, until he can hear nothing but his corazón beating like a hundred hummingbirds. The voices of his past enrage and urge him to the edge—hijo de la chingada, indio, negro.

La Quebrada will not settle for less than his soul, and he thrusts down on the balls of his feet and lets his dreams soar, whatever the cost. In mid-air he discovers that the water, the air, the rocks, and even the heat of the sun are joining together for his quest.

Who am I? The one who will both lie and fight to the death for truth, choosing the road that ends at a sheer cliff, who forges paths with a sharp machete, cutting myself, others, and the soul of madre tierra.

The one who cannot rest with made-up stories, decade-long delusions, left to mutter about my foolish, determined pursuit of love that reeks of failure and forgiveness.

19.
Aγ, Aγ, Aγ

SUSAN CALLED A FEW DAYS BEFORE MY MOM'S August visit, a tinge of anxiety in her voice.

"Mom couldn't get out of bed. Kaiser X-rayed her back, saw nothing, but concluded it was a pinched nerve. She got a cortisone shot. We have her in a wheelchair, as if things weren't hard enough. Good thing Violeta is here. She has more patience than all of us put together."

I sighed and tried to picture my mom in a wheelchair. "I bet she's scared. If it's a pinched nerve I can take her to Lori. A chiropractic adjustment is better than cortisone!" I had been going to see Lori for eleven years, having met her on my first soccer team when I moved to the Bay Area. I depended on her to realign me from the hazards of soccer games, car accidents, and child lifting.

Mom flew up, feeling much better and refusing to use the wheelchair. Driving her in the morning to Lori's office on San Pablo Avenue, we were quiet. My mind wanted to create a problem and I kept repeating my father's dicho: "There are no problems, only situations."

She refused my arm for support when we reached the stairs. "Come on, Linda. ¡No soy niña!"

Lori ushered us both into the exam room, and I helped Mom slowly lay down on the table. Lori had her move various parts of her body, watching for signs of pain, which my mother freely expressed with her signature "Ay, ay, ay." Her voice was strong, throwing out chispas that sparked.

"It isn't her back, it's her left hip," Lori said. "Did they take X-rays of her hips? They should have for a seventy-six-year-old woman. I won't do anything without seeing an X-ray first. But here is some roll-on pain reliever she can use for topical soreness."

I called Susan who confirmed the X-rays were only of her back. Lori referred me to a local facility and we left her office. I reached out and touched the dark, shiny leaves of the peace plants that lined the open-air hallway. When my father died, a friend had given me the same plant. A prolific grower, it had been divided many times in the ensuing five years.

I drove attentively to distract myself from the anxiety bubbling in my gut and pulled into the parking lot of Alta Bates Medical Center. My mother had already opened her door and slid her feet to the black asphalt. She was such a rascal. I calmly offered my hand, which she took reluctantly.

When they called her name, we left the waiting area and I helped her climb up on yet another table.

"What is thees for?" she asked.

"Your cadera. The pain."

"Oh, okay."

Her memory had continued to diminish since the Alzheimer's diagnosis a year and a half before. After the X-ray, we returned to my apartment and ate rice and carne, leftovers from the Peruvian restaurant of the night before. I had cringed in embarrassment when my mom told the waiter each time he came by how tough the meat was. When I left a good tip, Mom had balked, trying to take some of the money back.

"Oh, Linda. That's too much. The meat was tough."

Regardless of the meat quality, my mother was cheap when it came to tips. I usually surreptitiously added a few dollars when we went out and she paid. Tot had been the opposite, given his life as a waiter, and tipped very well.

I eased her onto the lower double bunk bed I had purchased, as I now shared a room with my twins when they were with me. While she rested, I sat down at my computer to check email and wait. The phone rang just as my mom stirred; I recognized Lori's calm voice. The radiologist had called in a report.

"There is a dark area in her hipbone suggestive of a malignant tumor. He can fax the report to me and you can pick it up today. He advised a bone scan as soon as possible." She switched her tone to friend and fellow soccer player. "I'm sorry, Linda."

The tears streamed down my face. I never wanted to pick up a phone again. Hanging up, I turned to watch Mom rustling around in my bed, trying to find a comfortable position. As I brewed a cup of manzanilla, I called Susan and Eddy to explain the basic details—suggestive, tumor, bone scan. Que camello. Once again grateful for their reconciliation a few months before, Susan and Fred agreed to drive up for the kids' sixth birthday party on Saturday. They'd drive back down to LA with Mom and me on Monday.

❧

Saturday was sunny at Aquatic Park. We hosted a big pachanga as Mom sat in her wheelchair, a pout playing on her lips most of the day. Eddy and his wife Shan-Yee brought my mom's youngest grandchild, Antonio, almost two years old, to sit on her lap. Throughout the day, the family anxiety was passed like a baton from Susan to Eddy to Fred to me by way of a look, a touch, or an unspoken word.

As I watched Teo and then Gina swing at the piñata with blindfolds, I marveled at their resilience. If they felt our worry, it didn't show as they celebrated their birthday. Teo ran with his friends on the soccer field. Gina sat quiet amid the activity, only her eyes moving from side to side while two red hearts outlined in black were painted on her left cheek. They generously allowed their small cousin Antonio to help them unwrap their gifts. They giggled as we sang: "Cumpleaños Feliz" followed by "Happy Birthday to You."

Kissing my niños good-bye at the end of the day, I told them how sorry I was to miss family camp with them and promised to bring them an LA treat. I woke up early and tense the next morning. Sitting cross-legged on the floor in my living room, I leaned my head back on the sofa, closing my eyes and holding my coffee with both hands to soak in the warmth and calm.

"Linda?"

I jerked my head up and rose. Placing my mother's coffee on the nightstand next to my father's picture, I carefully pulled her up to a sitting position.

"Ay, ay, ay," she said.

Ay, ay, ay was right. It signaled the time for her medications had arrived, and I headed towards my small bathroom. The floor iced my bare feet as I clasped the thin, nylon bag that held her pills. Zoloft for depression that had hounded her for five years, Aricept for the Alzheimer's, and extra strength acetaminophen. The prescription said two every four hours for relief of back pain. I returned to find my mom, delicately perched on the edge of the bed. Her eyes wandered around the room, taking in my small L-shaped bedroom.

"We have to get ready, Mom. They'll be here soon to pick us up."

Mom waved her hand as if to dismiss me. "No te afanes. So, what happened with you and Carolyn?"

I paused, contemplating the easiest response. "We didn't get along."

Her eyes crinkled in a sweet, conspiratorial way and her head tilted like the pajaritos on my bird feeder when they heard noise from inside the house. "Oh, come on, Linda. You can tell me."

"Ten—tus vitaminas." Handing her the four pills and water, I again noticed the similarity of our hands because of our mutually bad habits—pulling weeds with bare hands, washing dishes without gloves or enough soap, and rare manicures. I helped her pack last minute items in her well-traveled floral tapestry bag. Her brush went in, along with two pairs of knee-highs she had neatly folded into soft, square packets.

"¿Lo quieres?" I asked, holding out her black bufanda. She nodded and I placed it around her neck. She was shorter than before, her frailness accentuated by the weight loss of recent months. On my way to the bathroom I gazed at a picture hanging on my wall of her holding the twins when they were babies.

Her face was full six short years ago, the prominent cheekbones we shared more subtle. Her eyes were full of mirth behind the large glasses some older women prefer. Even her hair was stronger in tone, a vibrant brown that swirled in soft waves around her head. I did not look carefully at my mom before my father died, just felt her essence like we do with those that are so much a part of our lives. Now I was hyper-aware of every halting movement, every chin hair that sprouted, every stained blouse I cut up for the rag pile when she wasn't looking.

"¡Maldita sea!" Mom cried.

"What, Mom?"

The doorbell rang and I ran to open it. Susan and Fred stepped in, and I hurried back to Mamy. She was in the bedroom on her knees, her head at an angle down under the bed.

"Mis gafas. I can't find them!"

I scooched down with her and spied her glasses. They must have fallen after she finished with the morning paper. I helped her up carefully until I felt her forearm against my side, the signal my help was not welcomed.

Fred guided her gently into the back seat of the Jeep, wedging a pillow under her hip. It was my responsibility to keep her tranquila as Fred veered around the semis, Winnebagos, family vans, and occasional tumbleweeds. The I-5 was a highway full of anticipation, and now dread.

❧

Mom had a bone scan, and a day later Susan and I met alone with the oncologist.

"Your mother's original cancer, diagnosed and treated eleven years ago, has returned. It has spread to her bones," he said.

"I remember her first diagnosis," I said. "It was so early she needed only six weeks of radiation, not even a lumpectomy." The bullet we dodged in 1990 had ricocheted around the universe and lodged itself in her left hip.

My chest tightened and tears formed in my eyes. I didn't dare look at Susan, instead pressing my lips together and looking at the scan.

"You can see the many bright spots on the image, including her ribs, spine, and hips." He paused and then continued, "My suggestion, given her age, is to focus on pain management and quality of life. Radiation and chemotherapy have a minimal chance of success."

Susan and I looked at each other, no denial left in us, and sat back in our seats.

"How long?" I asked.

"I'd say two years," the doctor said, "but you can't really know." He looked down at his notes as if there was nothing more to say.

Susan and I both nodded. Two years would put us at August 2003. My kids would be turning eight. We thanked the doctor and walked out to her car. Driving home in task mode, we decided who to tell and when. Arriving at my mom's, we hugged and Susan drove home while I wandered out to the backyard to find some semblance of balance before knocking on Mom's bedroom door.

My parents were like their two aguacate trees, surviving heat and squirrels and bad pruning jobs, their large shiny leaves and two kinds of avocados finding their way to our salads year after year. My father had exercised, shifting from soccer to racquetball to golf, and he retired as soon as he reached sixty-five. My mom ate her homegrown orange a day, attended art classes at the Senior Center, and exercised at the gym. I remember going with her once—she flitted from machine to machine like a tiny colibrí from flower to flower, barely doing five or six reps before moving on. It was just an excuse for moving, for zipping around town with her personalized license plate that read "CHAVA," her Colombian nickname.

My parents had not lived near toxic dumps nor picked strawberries for hours in the unrelenting heat like many immigrants. Lard, which was common in many some recipes my mother learned to cook for her Mexican husband, was substituted with healthier options, and desserts were few and far between. They traveled to their two patrias and to Europe, Asia, and Alaska. Their children had college degrees and supported themselves and their families. There were no midnight calls from a bar or jail. Although we may have frustrated them with our choices of partners and jobs, we rarely missed holidays together.

Even though our family meals and conversations at the dinner table were not often playful or engaging, we did not eat in front of the TV, and we heated up tortillas every night no matter what was on the menu. We had gone to Disneyland every year and eaten perfectly ripe fruit off our own trees, along with dark, juicy blackberries off our brambles long before the word *organic* appeared on labels. Our upset stomachs were treated with yerba buena picked by Mom from her garden and boiled in a small stainless steel cazuela. I thought that meant my parents would not be so easily toppled by pulmonary fibrosis and now cancer. I was wrong.

§

I don't remember telling Mom about the cancer, but I must have. That moment is stored in my invisible room that holds a number of unpleasant memories. I do remember that her seventy-sixth birthday occurred three days after the diagnosis. We had doggedly moved forward with party plans and invited our long-time Colombian family friends, telling them beforehand of the diagnosis. Mom remained holed up in her room, refusing to leave her bed.

"Leave me alone! There is noteen to celebrate. Tell everyone to go home. I want to die."

A few brave souls knocked on the door, whispered her name, and entered timidly. She received them like a Leo, una leona with a big thorn in her hip. No one in my family liked being humored. We preferred to take it right on the chin. Each of us had our own brand of denial but we hated it from others.

"I can't believe it. First Rosendo and now Chava," said Gloria, "que barbaridad." She shook her head as she cut the cake into perfect squares and handed me a slice, even though I shook my head. "Coma, mi cielo. You'll feel better."

Susan kept busy brewing coffee and making sure everyone had a drink.

"Siéntate, Susanita." Enrique, Gloria's husband, motioned my sister to a chair. She relented and slid into a chair next to Fred; his strong fingertips rubbed her back. I sank into the circle of comfort and love that my mom refused.

Looking out at their yard, I recall my dad only exposed his vulnerability once, when he gave me his signed health care directive. He was counting on me to let him go with dignity. I didn't listen then. Now another letting go was before me, and I was better prepared to undertake this journey.

Mom was a muddle of heartache, and the man she had tied her wagon to was gone, abandoning their carefully crafted compromises and emotional debt repayment plan. Because I didn't know the depth and details of their agreements, I viewed her as the one abandoning her life and us by default. We were never a big part of her inner buoy.

I heard my mom crying those ragged-edged sobs from when Tot died. Gloria hurried into her room to offer solace. I pulled down my sleeves from doing dishes and followed her into Mamy's bedroom.

Part 4:
Fairness

Gina and Teo with cousins Arieti and Toño,
and the children of their oldest cousin Juan José;
celebrating 25th wedding anniversary of Tere and Victor, 2002

Four sisters, Acapulco, 2004

20.
My Heart Crumbles

AFTER RETURNING FROM MÉXICO, I HAD RAISED the issue of Tot's inheritance with Susan and Eddy, and our conversations continued amid Mom's decline. Susan had been formulating the idea of splitting it six ways, while Eddy initially only wanted to include Miguel.

"Why not our sisters? I don't think it's based on who sought him out or their financial need. It's a matter of what is fair and right. Just because you haven't met them and they stayed in México doesn't make them less worthy," I wrote, sending my response to his email with a hard push of the mouse. I didn't call because I might have bitten his head off, never a good idea with a González. His email response a few days later was brief and agreed to our plan. There was no big rush, however, because for now the money was Mom's.

Eddy and I met with an estate attorney. We raised the issue of dividing my father's inheritance six ways and he looked at us strangely, but agreed to see if the trust as written allowed for that. As Eddy, Susan, and I faxed forms and numbers back and forth, my belief that we had been treated the same revealed yet another secret.

"Susan, what did you get for college from Mom and Tot?" I asked.

"Nothing. I lived at home but I also worked. How about you?" she said.

"I definitely got some money and Mom paid off one of my small loans. What about your house?"

"I got a loan that I paid back. And you?" Susan said.

"I got some money, which went into Carolyn's house. No payback," I said.

"They re-financed their house to help Eddy buy his. And I don't remember him working through college, do you?"

"No, but I didn't pay attention. I know he had a gas credit card from them." I stopped. "I didn't realize we had been treated so differently." Another disappointment rumbled in my stomach after I hung up and began packing for my next trip to LA with my mom.

ॐ

I stepped through the security scanner in the San Jose Airport and heard a security guard asking, "Who is with this woman?" I turned to see him pointing to my mother.

"I am. What's the problem?" I said as I stuffed my computer back into its black case and hurried over to place my hands on the handles of her wheelchair.

It was November 2001, two months after 9/11. Recent security stories were *click click clicking* through my brain: The grandmother pulled off a plane and arrested for an off-handed comment. The mother who had her frozen breast milk taken from her. Post–9/11 security was in full force. Could we end up being a headline? *Mother and daughter arrested in San Jose Airport.*

She had passed through security before me because of her wheelchair. I had put her purse on the conveyor belt and pulled my laptop out to place it in a separate bin from my backpack. The Alzheimer's had progressed enough that mom no longer fought her wheelchair. In the beginning she would refuse: "No, I don't need this! ¡Déjame caminar!" I would let her walk haltingly, putting most of her weight on her right leg, as her left hip held the bone cancer that was slowly metastasizing throughout her shrinking five-foot frame. I was an early version of an emotional support animal, lowering any anxiety she felt when she forgot where we were or what we were doing.

Now I was grasping the wheelchair handles, thinking I might have to engage in some civil disobedience if things got ugly. The security guard had an unfriendly face, his hand hovering near the gun holster on his right hip. I touched her arm and motioned the guard to move away a few feet.

"She said she had a gun when we were checking her purse," the guard said.

A gun. I had to stop myself from the hysterical laugh that was trying to make its way up my throat. Mom was looking bewildered, clutching her purse.

"What is going on?" she asked.

"Momentito, Mamy." I turned to him. "She has Alzheimer's. She doesn't remember the 9/11 attacks *and* she has an odd sense of humor. She is just mad you were checking her purse."

He looked at me, and then looked, really looked at my mom, sitting in the wheelchair, her eyes darting from side to side. He saw what I saw: a thin, frail woman. A woman that did not have a gun.

"Can I ask why you checked her purse?"

"Something popped up on the X-ray," he said.

"Did you find anything?"

"No." He paused. "Oh, go on. Get to your plane." He leaned in. "This is no joke, lady. You need to keep her under control."

I laughed inside at that command. There was no controlling my mom pre- or post-Alzheimer's. Mamy was going to plan her own show, sell the tickets, and kick anybody out who did not laugh at her jokes about having a gun. That is, if she remembered.

There was no point in telling her not to make jokes about guns in airports. Just like I used to distract my twins from something I didn't want them to have when we traveled, that was the only approach that worked now with her.

Pushing her wheelchair and looking down at the top of her head, I remembered her reaction the last time I had taken her to get it dyed. I had whispered to the stylist, "Use a darker color." I decided to pick a hue closer to her original hair color. Mamy had looked in the mirror after it was done and exclaimed, "Oh, Linda. Theese ees horrible. Too dark. Que asco!" I had reluctantly agreed my idea failed. The darker color made her pale skin even starker in contrast—her profile closer to the outline of a Día de los Muertos sugar skull.

As I chattered away about quién sabe que and forced myself to keep a steady pace through the airport crowds, out of the corner of my eye I saw the guard following us until we disappeared down the airplane entry ramp. My breath remained shallow as the plane taxied to the runway and took off. I munched on one honey-roasted peanut after another as my mom flipped through a copy of yesterday's paper. When she finished, she started again from the beginning, her mind having erased the security guard, her cancer, her depression, and the headline news.

Her purse triggered the airport X-rays three more times. After this scene, I had learned to make sure her purse went through the X-ray last, so I could get through and distract her as they checked her purse.

"Ay mira Mamy, a pigeon got into the building—look at it flying up there" or "Are you hungry? Should we get a golosina and cafecito before getting on the plane?"

They finally found the mysterious weapon that my mother carried on to so many planes. It was a tiny pen-knife that had slipped in underneath the lining of the purse.

After the trauma of the airport, I happily sat in mom's swivel chair in her office and located the tax paperwork amid her files. I recycled the bills and files that were outdated and found a spiral notebook full of my mom's handwriting. Stuffing it in my purse, I kept searching for financial clues. The information about the re-financing to help Eddy was there. It made a mockery of what Susan had said after Tot's funeral about treating us the same as Eddy. My head felt full of hot steam.

I stomped into my mother's bedroom and confronted her as she watched the news.

"Why did you help Eddy so much with his house when you made Susan pay back her loan?"

"Oh, Linda. What do you care? He needed the money."

"And Susan didn't? Why do you treat him like a consentido?" I said.

"Ju don know notin." Her lips jutted out and she turned up the TV volume.

I took my anger to the kitchen and phoned Susan. "What are we going to do? We can't deal with being fair for our other siblings and ignore what happened right here."

Susan's response was muted and weary. The whole thing just irked me. Raising a boy and a girl had made me attentive to how the world so easily favored males. I thought I was passing on a tradition of fairness. This brought to mind one of my father's dicho: "You don't hate anything, you dislike it." Not today, Tot. Today I hated this.

Susan and I agreed to cool down before talking to Eddy. I packed the paperwork in my carry-on and was glad my mom had no memory of my outburst.

While waiting for my plane to board, I pulled out the notebook I had stumbled on at my mom's. It was small with a plastic orange cover. I opened it and began reading:

> *But you couldn't be lonely, you have a husband.*
> *But you couldn't be bruised, I didn't hit you that hard.*
> *But you couldn't be depressed, you have good kids.*

It was my mother's handwriting, but there was nothing in my experience of her that resonated with this voice. Did she really write this? If not, why would she copy it and from where?

> *I want to keep moving, but I am very still. I am*
> *not fully present. I fill my head with thoughts*
> *when I am alone. I want to have a silent mind.*
> *Someday, not too far away, I'll be able to put*
> *aside all my thoughts, I know, when I am dead.*
> *What an awful thought, but it is my only hope.*
> *Life for me doesn't have much meaning anymore.*
> *My home is so quiet. When I enter the rooms*
> *that my kids once occupied, I try to remember*
> *their faces, to hear their voices. And then I feel*

that my heart crumbles, that I don't have enough
air to breathe.

I wept quietly, seeing words that illuminated her vulnerability, her clarity, and her suffering. Even if she had copied some of the phrases and written some herself, they rang true. I closed my eyes. We had never talked at that level and now we never would.

My mom's last words in the notebook were:

I am spiritual(ly) dead. I don't have faith. If I am
dead don't cry for me, you should celebrate.

One year she hand-sewed all three of us cloth dolls. The compassion and care she couldn't show us directly was in each detailed stitch of those dolls. The writing I found indicated she had some awareness of her struggles:

I should never be a mother. Yes, I was good at
changing diapers, having their food on time on
the table, but when they grew up I wanted every-
thing perfect for them. I know I don't understand
their way of life, their feelings. How could I if I
never understood myself?

She did what she felt good at and skirted what made her feel inadequate.

Once safely home, I opened my novel, but my mind kept wandering to my mom's words, which had no date to mark them and no other entries. My intuition said she wrote this when we were in our mid to late twenties. Susan was the last to leave the house in 1982. That could very well be the timing, although the words also resonated with her frame of mind when Tot died.

ஃ

Maintaining a ragged meditation schedule some mornings, I reminded myself to stick to the basics. I nurtured forgiveness for, of all people, myself. It was not wrong to focus on awakening to my life and understanding what unconditional love felt like, tasted like, could be like. I had plenty of time to practice with those around me as I plowed through the shit that was la vida now in my familia. My mom was coming up in a week for her every other month visit so I scheduled a weekend trip to write and rejuvenate.

As I wrote over the next two days, the voices inside became loud, screaming banshees, and I turned on them: "Why should I be any less brave than my children who are making all kinds of friends and exploring their world?"

I had been told to shut up and tone down for years, starting with the man and woman who raised me with their own fire. They saw in me their own image, their own early yearnings to be free. They never really had the chance to turn their spark into a steady flame that warmed rather than scorched, and inadvertently snuffed each other out while also feeding off each other's blaze.

Their children reacted differently to this environment. I raged outside my body, screaming, ripping dresses, and once being dunked in the pool by my mom in her desperate attempt to cool my heat. Susan and Eddy had been silent observers, deciding that fire was too dangerous and it was better to walk the other way, banish their voice, and swallow their tears.

I returned to my small apartment refreshed and welcomed my mom for her week-long visit.

"What is that smell?" she sniffed, stopping at the doorway.

"It's sage, Mom. It helps cleanse the air."

"You Northern Californians are such weirdos."

There it was, the machete I knew so well. I smiled. What, por dios, had she toiled for all those years to have her children be such oddballs? She headed for the bedroom, ready for a nap.

"What is deese?" Mom picked up a square laminated music box, opened it to hear the notes of "The Wind Beneath My Wings." I put her bag down and thought about Evelyn, the woman who had given me this gift several years ago.

Carolyn had organized a Grand Canyon river rafting trip. I had embraced river rafting as well as kayaking, attending a river guide school in my mid-thirties. I became a volunteer guide, and also took my family and friends on the South Fork of the American river. I was taught to "rig for a flip," tying everything down on the raft in case the boat flipped over. It was a reminder to not get arrogant and ever think our boat skills controlled Mother Nature.

I had been river rafting for ten years and was rowing Latisha, a paraplegic woman, down the river. Evelyn, the staff person accompanying us, was terrified of the rapids. She took several puffs from her inhaler at a stop before the bigger rapids due to her anxiety. I was glad I had an assistant guide, Josh, whose job was to help me keep both women safe.

I approached a rapid called Satan's Cesspool with less than my usual trepidation. The boat was heavy, more solid than a paddleboat due to the metal frame that held my wooden plank seat and two long oars. One minute I was in the boat, smiling as the raft photo people took our picture. The next I was underwater, stunned by this literal turn of events. We had rigged for a flip and we would see how well our knots held.

I looked for Evelyn, knowing Josh would have rescued Latisha as we had discussed earlier. Evelyn was underneath the boat in the air cavity and I hauled her out. She wouldn't let go of the boat and I wouldn't let go of her, so our momentum carried us down the following rapid, called Son of Satan. The rocks bumped roughly across my body, but I needed to stay with her. She was my responsibility and more helpless than Latisha, who I had spotted safely stashed on shore, laughing and giving high fives to Josh.

I pulled the boat to the shore with some help from other guides and helped Evelyn lay down on the sandy shore.

"Thank you so much," she said to me after she had caught her breath. We all decided the best course of action was to switch up the boat so we could fulfill her request to stay with me. I held Evelyn and soothingly talked her through the rest of the trip.

Evelyn hugged me one more time at take-out. "You saved my life."

The river, like life, always ran the show, teaching us the value of reading the current situation and having a Plan A, B, and C. "Read it and run" was the basic mantra by which we guides lived. We could let change sweep us out of the current or we could figure out how to get back into harmony with the flow.

As I stood next to my mom, I knew we were moving toward an inevitable flip, and I would stay with her no matter what. I hoped my knots, some of which I was still tying, would hold.

Opening the music box, I put my arm lightly around my mom's bony shoulders, now that she allowed a bit more affection as the Alzheimer's progressed. "A friend gave me this, Mom. Do you like the song?"

❧

After Mom returned home, I reflected on what I had learned that day on the river and what knots were loose in my family. The inheritance loomed large huge; I focused my attention there. I called Eddy and requested we count gifts over $5,000 from Mom and Tot during our lifetime as part of our inheritance. He agreed and came up with a complex calculation with columns and formulas for all six children. This laid the foundation for an inheritance split that took into account the unequal monetary gifts. We were going against our parents' written will, literally. There were no simple solutions to the "situations" that flipped boats and families into the unknown. But that did not mean there weren't solutions. Languages are never in a state of purity; they are constantly transformed by the environment. So too with families.

I have had to forgive all of my siblings for any number of acts. I have no doubt they have had to decide whether to forgive me or not. The only other option was to judge an act as being unforgivable, and where did that leave us if we wanted to find what was good, what was gold, indestructible and precious? I had to allow for space and time to do its work, to refine truths or abandon them.

20.
What Do You Need to Say?

M Y NEXT VISIT TO LA WAS ALMOST ENJOYABLE. Mom's current phase was sweet and a bit vapid. Her depression was like an espresso bean coated over with the milk chocolate of memory loss. After letting me in and walking to the kitchen, she caught sight of her rose bushes in the backyard. They grew outside the sliding glass doors covered with bars and inexpensive sun protection sheets.

"Look how beautiful are the roses." She and I had the same habit of translating our second language with the syntax from our first.

I dove into cleaning out the kitchen from six years of neglect, and the sense of a definitive accomplishment cheered me. The top of the refrigerator—sticky and dusty—shone again as my rag, one of my mom's old, stained shirts, gathered grime within its folds.

I added a second bulb to the low hanging light fixture. I transferred drawers full of half cleaned silverware, plates and bowls into the dishwasher. Bug infested flour, dried up herbs and putrid sesame oil were in the bag that I tossed triumphantly into the black trash can near the front of the house. The malfunctioning microwave and oven were beyond my scope, so I earmarked them for Eddy's next visit.

I managed a rueful smile, as if the orderly cabinets could bring stability to our lives. Just to confirm my delusion, I showed my mom the clean kitchen, and her response was a terse: "So whawt."

That's what my mom said when she suspected someone was judging her, and today I saw it as simply two words, rather than an indictment against me or my efforts. After collecting the stained placemats off the table, I headed for the washing machine but instead tossed them in the bathroom basura. Cumplida.

"Come on Mom, let's go shopping."

"You're so skeeny," she told me with a nod of approval while we drove to Bed Bath & Beyond.

"So are you," I replied.

She chortled.

The key remarks as we drove the next day to the market, to the beach, and to my sister's house were about how green and pretty the trees were, how the houses and apartments were clean with no basura, and how the neighborhood hadn't been spoiled.

She was into tape. Susan said she taped holiday cards up on the walls. A picture of my children was taped to her bedroom wall. What particularly caught my eye was a chair in the computer room. It had three rows of brightly colored tacks pushed in along the top of the back of the cloth chair. I looked up at the corkboard above the chair and smiled at what she had done.

The board was full of pictures of the family over the last fifteen years or so. Within these photos were sprinkled a few comics and a picture sent to her of the past four Republican presidents. The pictures were carefully taped to the corkboard and to each other.

I mentioned her handiwork and she beamed. "¿Mucho mejor, don't you think? I took out the pins—they were ugly." She was cheerful and childlike in her delight, with the distinction that her capacity was in a downward spiral.

On my last night before returning home, I set up the projector and pulled out sixteen years of slides. My dad had thinned them out before dying. His original, perfectly formed labels had been crossed out with new writing and far less carousel boxes. I set up the screen and darkened the living room, something we hadn't done since before my father's death.

As we traveled through the slides, I pulled out the ones that awakened something inside my memories. I kept a paper near me and asked my mom questions about people I didn't know or locations I couldn't identify before she lost that part of her memory. As glad as I was for gathering this information, it was taxing. I woke up the next morning feeling like I needed to sleep a few more hours. Instead, I packed my pajamas and toiletries into my carry-on and kissed my mom goodbye. Susan drove me to the airport, a route we both knew far too well.

৵

I woke up in my Berkeley apartment a month later feeling something was wrong. My mom was with me again on one of our regular bimonthly turnarounds. I eased down the round, metal stairs of the bunk bed above my sleeping mom. My body felt twenty pounds heavier, as if professionals had pummeled me without leaving visible bruises. I stumbled to the bathroom on puffy feet. Bending my arms and knees caused a dull ache to radiate out. Nothing in my history helped me digest this. The closest I got was my sister's description of total body soreness after her first marathon, an easy A + B = C causation.

As my mom slept peacefully, I dialed my doctor's number.

"For same day appointments, press two."

"Hello? I need an appointment today. Yes. Dr. Logan. She's on vacation? A Nurse Practitioner? Sure. Eleven a.m. is fine."

After a light breakfast of my mom's favorite English muffin with mantequilla y mermelada, I drove her the two blocks to Carolyn's. My mom and I walked haltingly up the stairs. I said my hellos and goodbyes to Carolyn and the kids in rapid succession before anyone noticed my hands.

The Nurse Practitioner Becky McGrath assessed my symptoms. Her monotone voice and dry, almost prissy manner made me miss Dr. Logan, whose genuineness helped me trust her in a setting I avoided. The visit ended with a referral for blood work and a suggestion to rest and take ibuprofen for pain and swelling.

My symptoms slowly subsided over twenty-four hours and Eddy picked up Mom for a few days before she returned to Los Angeles. My friend Miriam came by at nine on Monday to drive me to my follow-up appointment.

"Linda González?"

We rose together and followed the nurse into a waiting room. The nurse practitioner Becky entered shortly. Her glasses perched on the end of her nose, she sat down without a word of greeting.

"Your blood work is in. I consulted with Dr. Gerhardt and he agrees your elevated ANA, which stands for Antinuclear Antibody, along with the flare you experienced last week, is indicative of lupus. Lupus is an autoimmune disease, fairly common with African American and Latin women. Do you have a lot of fat in your diet?"

I shook my head no, the word refusing to enter my body. Lupus. This was the worst-case scenario according to my research, the disease with the most severe consequences, including painful joints and overwhelming fatigue treated with steroids for the rest of the patient's life.

"Linda?" Miriam's voice broke through, pulling me back into the hard plastic seat. "She is asking about your family. Is there anyone with an autoimmune disease?"

"No." I shook my head again. "No one. The best thing my parents gave me were their healthy genes."

"Do you exercise?" Becky asked.

"I play soccer twice a week, run around and bike with my kids, do some river rafting and sea kayaking. I take a tai chi class once a week and go to salsa lessons every couple of weeks."

She appeared stumped, biting the end of her pen. "So, you eat well and exercise. How about stress? Flares can be caused by stress."

"My mom was visiting, but I felt fine beforehand and I feel fine now, just a little tired."

"Oh, yeah. Mothers can be a pain." Becky looked up in my direction, the slightest emotion in her voice.

"She's dying of cancer." I looked at her with anger, but she just kept writing, ignoring my words.

"Minimizing stress is critical to avoid flares. If you are in too much pain, you may need to come in for steroids."

Oh no. I stretched out my fingers. Steroids? No way. Miriam and I stood up and walked down the hallway with the nurse practitioner Becky trailing us.

"You don't fit the profile," Becky said, "Maybe it's karma—maybe you killed somebody in your past life."

I kept walking, pushing open the door and hurrying to the elevator. "Miriam, did you hear what she said?"

"Yeah. I can't believe she said that!"

"What's up with these people? I didn't fit in the box, so it's karma. My only bad karma was getting her instead of Dr. Logan."

I phoned my naturopath only to find she was on vacation as well. Summer was not a good time to get sick, apparently. Not knowing what else to do, I decided to keep up with my regular exercise and tai chi classes for the two weeks until I could see Dr. Wang.

The next day I dressed in my new black pants and drove to tai chi in my friend Terry's backyard. I kept losing the movement sequence after two or three in a row. My body was taking me down when I needed it most: when I had to care for my mom and make sure my kids had a great birthday party even if their moms weren't together. I lost the moves again. I looked over at Terry to see if I could mimic her.

"Linda, 'step forward and punch with fist' follows 'parts horse's mane.'" Vivian's voice held a mild note of irritation.

"This is not working for me." I looked at the teacher, a woman I had admired when classes began a month ago. "I need you to slow it down. I have never done this before."

"But the rest of the class is following my pace," she said calmly.

"I don't care about the rest of the class!"

"What's the matter, love?" Terry's voice interceded, her kind tone breaking through my guard.

"I can't concentrate." My friend came over but I brushed aside her attention. "I'm sorry. I have to go."

I practically ran down the driveway and drove home. *I have lupus.* I said it over and over again, at each stoplight, when I turned the car off, as I put the key into my door-knob. Kicking my shoes off hard, I barely missing the vase of irises and sunflowers I had bought myself earlier as a treat.

Jumping into the shower, I watched the water stream off my arms, breasts, and thighs. Most days and nights, I loved my body: firm, supple, bruised, full of beauty marks. I heated up some arroz con pollo and settled onto my couch with *The Last Report on the Miracles at Little No Horse*.

Two weeks later I drove to Sausalito to see Dr. Wang, a naturopath I had established a relationship with six months earlier, at the same time I chose Dr. Logan to be my general practitioner. It had been one of my efforts towards self-care to find health care practitioners for myself since my mother's diagnosis.

"Oh, no. This is not lupus. I have excellent results with patients with an elevated ANA and thyroid antibodies." Dr. Wang's voice was full of certainty. "Let me put you on a program and we'll repeat the blood work in three months."

"Are you sure?" I asked.

"Absolutely." She lowered her head and wrote out a list of supplements.

I sat on the loveseat in her spacious office, looked out-side at the sunlight playing on the oak trees that lined the street and cried. I was mired in pills: My pills, my mom's pills, and even Teo's Chinese herb pills that made his asthma a non-issue. I reached for the tissue box and blew my nose.

Dr. Wang looked up. "What is it?"

"I keep making lists in my journal about self-care and spending time with friends. It's summer and I have been river rafting exactly once. My dentist says I am wearing my teeth down with my clenching so now I wear a $400 mouth guard at night—how sexy is that?"

Dr. Wang leaned in, her eyes full of concern. "You have been through a lot. The throat is your voice. There is a reason your body is sending antibodies there. What do you need to say?"

"I can't say anything fully, because everyone around me feels ready to crack. Everyone but my mom, who is the *most* fragile. She's becoming all lightness and cheer as the Alzheimer's erases her 'Woe is me' files, but her body is full of cancer. I don't want to lose her, don't want her to forget who I am, cannot bear to think about the last time she will say my name."

"And you have friends and activities that heal you. Everything can't be centered on your family and your mother—"

"But it is. I got what I wanted. Because if there is one thing that Latina means, it is Mom and familia. No matter how much my father's death hurt, it is my mom's death that will kill me."

Dr. Wang sat still as I wiped mascara off my face.

"Can you find a middle path that helps you *and* your family feel better?" she asked. "Because you need your body to heal. *You* are the one who can get better."

"I know. I promise to think about it."

Accepting the brown paper bag full of pills, homeopathic drops, and directions for castor oil packs for my knees after soccer games, I contemplated her words as I made my way to my car. As I drove home the gas tank indicator slid into the red. I wondered how far I could go before running out of gas. In the past, I had pushed too far several times and had had to hoof it to a nearby gas station with my plastic gas can in hand. The warning light still triggered my gambling reflex. I pulled off the highway and filled up my tank.

"Susan!" I startled my sister later that day with my urgency on the phone.

"How's your health?" she asked.

"I'm fine. My naturopath says it's not lupus! I just have to take as many pills as Mom for a while and eliminate the little wheat and caffeine left in my diet."

"Have you talked to your other doctor?"

"No, but I have an appointment with her in three days so we'll see what she says," I replied.

"I still think you should take it easy."

"I am not sick! Didn't you hear me?"

"Sure, you *and* mom are not sick. I hear you. Gotta go. Love you."

"Love you too."

Looking at the official meditation zafu I had bought a month ago, I sat on it gingerly, the buckwheat filling making a soft crunching noise. *Healing has its own timeline*, I told myself firmly as I got up after a mere five minutes.

ॐ

Walking down the hallway where my karma had been diagnosed, my eyes darted left and right. I did not want to run into "that woman." Dr. Logan knocked on the exam room door a few minutes later and entered, her dark cornrows resting on her shoulders, her ready smile as appealing as at our first appointment.

"Hello. It looks like you came in for some symptoms and got blood work done. How are you feeling?"

"Okay. I haven't had any more flares, and I am on some supplements and homeopathic remedies from my naturopath. She feels she can work to address the deep-rooted reasons for my symptoms. She doesn't think it's lupus."

Dr. Logan looked at my file briefly. "She's right. You don't have lupus. The diagnosis is wrong. In fact . . ." She took her pen and moved it back and forth across the word lupus on my chart. "There. You have an autoimmune disease in the arthritic family—that's all we can say. You need to watch out for heart palpitations, fatigue, and night sweats. Otherwise, follow your naturopath's plan and we can repeat the blood work in six months."

৯

My dream to live in more of a community setting erupted unexpectedly near the end of the summer, when I bought a piece of Berkeley property with four units with a friend's ex-husband. My large three-bedroom, two-bath home full of light and promise was a huge jump from the tiny apartment I had lived in for a year. It was less than a mile from my twins' other home—a big consideration. In a matter of two months I had become a homeowner and a landlord. This house meant I had a big view, light in every room, a community. This house meant I could host guests easily, loosen my movements, and breathe despite my dying mom and dissolving nuclear family.

The co-owner occupied the apartment on the ground floor. His son was in my kids' class. A friend moved into my home temporarily with his daughter, another classmate. My kids hopped around like two bunnies when they came over, happy to be near their friends.

While I was feeling slightly more energized and relieved, my mom's short-term memory continued to slowly ebb out like a slow leak on a tire, and Susan's voice held an edge of fretfulness and anger that was becoming a permanent fixture. Her name would pop up on my cell phone and I dreaded the heaviness of her words. It made me want to run to my small balcón and wrap myself up like a giant cocoon in the large multi-striped hammock from Colombia. I had bought it during a visit with my mom and Susan in August. It had been a chance to let Mom visit her patria one last time and allow her familia to see her. Even though they struggled to accept the seriousness of her illness due to her cheerful demeanor, it was part of Susan's and my closing ritual.

To give Susan a two-week break, I invited Miguel to come up with Mom and Violeta in late September. Mom thought Violeta was included because she was Miguel's girlfriend. She had no idea we paid Violeta to stay with her during the day and make sure she stayed home and took her pills. I worked out where three more people would sleep while singing my good night songs to Teo y Gina, my mind already sneaking out their door while my voice finished up "la luna ya aparecio, es hora de dormir, es hora de descansar."

"Hola, hermanita." Miguel bounded up the stairs with Mom and Violeta following slowly behind.

I hugged him, his light blue button-down shirt with large white flowers a reflection of his spirit. While Miguel and I shared no discernible physical traits, we shared an internal imp that aligned us both to my mother.

"¡Don't yell, hombre!" Mom chastised him, a playful note in her voice.

Violeta reached out to take her arm at the doorway and she accepted. They were a funny triangle, but it worked.

"Ay, sí, she comes to visit me when she has had enough of Miguel," Mom said with a chuckle.

Miguel helped me redo the backyard by hiring day laborers every morning to tackle the backyard brambles. Like my mom, I couldn't stand an untended garden and I wanted the yard to be useable by the children. I liked giving Miguel his due and money for work that needed to be done.

Along with a new retaining wall in the front yard, the piles of concrete and bushes in the backyard slowly disappeared and a load of rolled up strips of green turf was delivered. Eddy came over and helped Miguel and I lay out the grass. We posed for a picture proudly, holding our shovels like spears just used in battle. It was rare footage of us relaxed and together.

Mom meanwhile was quite silly, throwing wadded up papelitos at us when we weren't looking and giggling as if we wouldn't know it was her. I now had a teenager in the house disguised as my mom. We all laughed, enjoying her playfulness after so many years of her morose behavior.

Two weeks later, Mom climbed carefully into the big cab of Miguel's truck and they drove off. There was some measure of peace in all the untangling of Tot's two familias, even though my mom, who was a central character and who had known more than we wanted to believe, understood nothing about the present chapter. I was worried about the next year, as I had noticed Miguel and Violeta shared my bedroom but had set up a separate bed on the floor. If their relationship ended, the current set-up might crumble as had the others before.

෨

In October, I headed to México with my kids, ostensibly to celebrate Tere and Victor's twenty-fifth wedding anniversary. In truth, Miguel had informed me that Rosita's younger son Juan Carlos, who I had met for only five minutes on my first visit, had been killed in a freak accident a few months before. His car had stalled and he was walking down a highway when a truck passed by with a heavy metal bar sticking out. It hit him in the head and he died instantly. He was only thirty-two.

We took off just a month and a half after buying and moving into the new home. Once we landed in the airport, the kids ran ahead after we passed through customs. I chased them, forgetting to zip up my money pouch after hurriedly sticking the passports back inside. As we reached to bottom of the ramp leading to the luggage, the pouch flipped over and cash spilled out.

As part of our six children money talks, we had agreed to give my sister Tere an advance of her inheritance. I was on my hands and knees grabbing at thousands of dollars, yelling at the kids to help me. Nothing like stepping into another country and flashing your lana como una gringa. After zipping it all up, we gathered our two suitcases and walked out to find our familia waiting, almost one and a half years from our last visit.

The kids were less shy when Tere and Arieti met us con abrazos.

Tere and Victor gave me their room to stay in again and I avoided la abuela's eyes when I entered the room. Despite the fifteen years difference in age, the cousins se llevaron bien, with Toño letting Teo hold his BB gun as I watched cautiously from the doorway. It mattered to me that we build a sturdy foundation with this generation.

The fiesta for Tere and Victor took place in a large community room within the apartment complex where Rosita lived. I stayed close to my oldest hermana, who mostly sat quietly. Having shared so little of our important life passages, this was a time to share the sadness and the joy.

Before the fiesta I spoke with Arieti in her kitchen. She was brusquer than I had ever seen her, telling me she didn't consider my father her grandfather. He had hurt her mother and that was that. I understood that protectiveness, had begun to feel it more in my own relationship with my mother. No matter how much we overcome, we have soft spots that warrant safeguarding.

I listened to Rosita's sorrow, her body laden with the heavy loss of her son Juan Carlos. There was so little to do with our collective sadness except let it sit alongside us.

"Un foto."

I was heading back in with Gina and Teo from the small playground when I saw Rosita standing next to her oldest and now only son, Juan José. Racing inside, I brought my camera out and posed them, their heads leaning in. I then gathered the gaggle of cousins for a photo. How little we know about our families when childhood photos are taken.

We left with more ties and the hope that the happier memories could offset the many years of pain. Teo slept for most of the plane trip while Gina and I read until the captain informed us we were nearing Oakland airport.

Two days after returning I spoke with Susan on a Saturday, eager to share about mi casa and mi viaje. Friday had been our weekly "special night" and Gina had stayed with me while Teo stayed with Carolyn. We did this so they could do their favorite things without having to negotiate with their sibling.

"Hey, I'm listening to surround sound Juanes."

"That's nice," she said. "I took Mom to the doctor yesterday and they changed her prescription so we waited one hour in the pharmacy and then the traffic was horrible. Violeta was late getting to the house on the bus so I got home late for a dinner for one of Fred's co-workers. He had already begun drinking and I yelled at him and stayed in my room for half an hour to calm down enough to go be the cheerful wife."

My right eye was twitching by the time her monologue ended. I thought about my Saturday. Gina would rouse herself around ten and we would make pancakes together, her favorite breakfast. I would then ride bikes with her to Carolyn's home, where she would stay for the rest of the weekend with Teo. I had no plans in place other than to water the new lawn and go shopping at the farmers' market.

"Can you rest today?" I asked.

"Rest? The laundry I meant to do yesterday is waiting for me and Steven has a wrestling match. Violeta is going to visit her sister so Fred went to get Mom for the day."

"I'll be down the weekend before Thanksgiving for Victor Villaseñor's Snow Goose celebration. Maybe I can bring Mom back up with me," I said.

"Okay. I hear Fred pulling in the driveway. Love you."

"Love you too." I placed the receiver down and leaned against the cool wall of my dining room, knowing I could never do enough at a distance of over three hundred miles to ease Susan's day-to-day angustia.

Walking down my stairs and around my new neighborhood, I stopped to touch the smooth, bare branches on the trees, foretellers of winter and rain. I ended up sitting in our lush backyard grass, eyeing the young fruit trees we had planted the weekend before, my two favorites being the albaricoque and the aguacate. My hope was they would someday be as fruitful as the ones in my parents' backyard. I climbed the thirteen stairs to my second-floor landing. Continuing to the third floor, I calculated in my mind what changes to make to my office space to accommodate a bed and furniture.

My heart palpitated as I picked up the framed photo of my mom at her birthday celebration in Colombia in August. Susan had tried to take care of both Mom and me, making sure she rested and I avoided caffeine and wheat as I recuperated from my stress flare.

Susan was tired and spent and yet she kept on with the grind as older sisters do sin pensarlo. I wondered what my own voice would sound like in three months at my forty-fifth birthday. Would I have a permanent edge like Susan from being Mom's primary caregiver?

I picked up the phone, took a breath, and pressed redial, ready to find out.

22.
Pasado Mañana

SUSAN HAD EASILY AGREED TO HAVE MOM LIVE with me full-time. She had come up after we celebrated Thanksgiving in LA. Always a fan of Craigslist, I sold my rarely used weight bench and small trampoline to clear out the space next to my office set-up. Simultaneously, I searched for a bed, nightstand, and chest of drawers, taking care to measure my dimensions so that carrying these up two flight of stairs would be worth it.

A key component to adding my mom into an already packed calendar was to ask my twice a month housecleaner Dalia if she had time to become a stealth caretaker. She did. I explained this meant doing light cleaning and sometimes cooking while she mostly made sure my mom was safe and entertained. I also found an Alzheimer's Day Center and arranged for my mom to be picked up and dropped off two days a week.

"When am I going home?" Mom asked after three days of what she thought was her "visit" in my house.

"Pasado mañana," I responded casually to her in what would become my mantra in the coming months. Depending on the circumstances, I added a few more details. "You're driving down with me" or "Vamos por avión" or "We're taking the bus down with the kids," all of which were true at one point or another.

Of the lessons that stuck with me from school, one from a high school English teacher, Miss Crampton, served me best in acclimating to my mom's dementia. The key component was the omission of a piece of true information rather than the intentional addition of false information. I have no idea why she shared it with us, but I had become very grateful for what I dubbed "The Acceptable Lie." As I dug into the family secrets, I saw that my parents had been masters of this form of communication.

"Pasado mañana" was my equivalent of "not today," which was true. Mom was not going home today. She was resting on the edge of a bed she did not know had been bought specifically for her, tucked in the corner of the upstairs open-air space, the bruises on her face turning yellow.

My mom had fallen a week earlier on the way to Taco Bell a few blocks from her house; her hands stretching out to protect her, her face colliding with the pavement in shock. She looked, said Susan, like a boxer who lost more rounds of the bout but won the fight on a knockout. The fall did not break her bones or her spirit. She sat in the emergency room, asking my sister repeatedly: "Why am I here?"

When told why, she remarked teasingly: "Violeta tripped me. She put her foot out to trip me. She wanted my taco!"

❧

I was living with my mother for the first time in twenty-seven years. When I had ended my relationship with Carolyn, Mom told Susan: "Linda says she is going to live with me." During each visit she peppered me with one persistent question said as if it were a command, "You're coming to live with me, no?"

I'd smile and say gently, "Ay, Mamy, how can I leave my kids?"

Mom would smile, accepting the truth until her mind would circle back to the same soundtrack. "You're coming to live with me, no?"

I brought Mom the newspaper and sat down at my desk to check email, five feet away from her. Her new bed was perfect, with the same remote control as her bed in LA. It allowed her to raise her head or feet and accommodate hours of newspaper reading or TV watching. She seemed unfazed by the trampa. We had woven our distinct lives together, with her heading off for the Alzheimer's Day Program that we called "The Senior." She thought she was "volunteering," one of the multiple re-designs of reality shaped and re-shaped each day to help us both.

છ

For my forty-fifth birthday, a few months after Mom joined the household, I asked my salsa teacher, Philip, to come and give everyone lessons. He had been coming to my house once a week to grease my dancing wheels. Attending a class would require too much coordination and salsa fueled my energy. After the lessons for my fiesteros in my living room, he nodded to me and I turned off the lights, leaving only the strand of red chili peppers glowing. Besides framing the three dining room windows, it illuminated the shadowed people sitting on the sofa right below, including my mom and my brother Eddy, who had now gone for many years as Rosendo.

Philip took me in his arms and led me into a cross body lead followed by a right outside turn and then a left inside turn. By then I had forgotten the crowd, tuned instead to the music and the feel of my soles sliding easily across the wooden floor in the hands of a wonderful partner. Blue pill boxes, laundry, and the shadow of death smoking a cigarette just outside my front door faded into the background. After a quick bow, I meandered in and around my new fans to find the mojito I had left on the bookshelf near my mom.

"Wow, Linda. I deedn't know you danced!" My mom was smiling.

I sat down on the low table in front of her, careful to keep my legs closed. "I'm still new at this, but I figured it is never too late, que no?"

Susan came over and tapped me on the shoulder. "You always liked performing, didn't you? You and Mom."

"*You* were the one who danced Ballet Folklórico!" I retorted. But inside I knew she was making a point about our everyday loudness that easily stung her quieter soul.

"This is your last birthday party with Mom. Maybe we should take a picture," Susan whispered.

The air was sucked out of my lungs. Fun seemed to have a maximum five-minute limit these days. I nodded and wended my way to the kitchen where I kept the rectangular blue plastic pill holder. Opening up the container labeled *SAT eve*, I detoured to the mojito pitcher, refilling my glass before walking back to my mom with pills number five, six, and seven y un vaso de agua.

In the morning, Mom drove with me to my chiropractic appointment. I had been rear-ended a few weeks before. They only looked at the light turn green and did not see I had not yet driven forward. This appointment was for me. It was the first time Mom was entering Lori's office with the hip pain that turned out to be cancer.

I twisted my neck to feel for pain. "How's your mom?" Lori asked as she examined my posture.

"Oh, she's living with me now. My mom is in the Kaiser hospice program. I have appointments with the social worker, the nurse, and the art therapist who does creative projects with the kids, not to mention check-ups with her two doctors. And there's the estate attorney."

"Can you come in at the same time next week?"

I looked at my appointment book. "No, Mom has her monthly Aredia Intravenous treatment. That takes a whopping two to three hours plus travel time. Thursday is the soonest I can come."

The next appointment at Kaiser shook me badly. Dr. Albright expressed satisfaction at Mom's health, intimating she could live for quite some time. It was April, one year and nine months from the two-year prognosis. I chuckled at my absurd attachment to the initial timeline, as if I was meting out the gas in my tank so that I was near empty when she died.

❧

Over Memorial Day weekend, Carolyn had the kids so only Mom and I were home. I was watching my mom knit a growing beige bufanda as we enjoyed a movie, our feet propped up on the sofa recliner. She shivered.

"¿Tienes frío?" I covered her skinny legs with my thick, wool Colombian ruana. It had warmed me for ten years, a gift from my Colombian cousin, Maria Elisa, on her last visit here.

Mom could sit for hours in relative stillness, nestled on the couch like this as we watched movies neither of us cared much about. My mind photographed the four feet propped up, our toes toward heaven.

Monday dawned with Mom's sharp cries of pain.

"¡Ay, ay, ay, caray! Me duele mi cadera," she exclaimed.

That very same hip had alerted us that her journey was beginning its final chapter. On Tuesday, I called Michele, the hospice nurse, telling her I was giving Mom Percocet every four hours with no evidence of relief.

On Wednesday evening, I upped the time-released morphine and did so again on Thursday morning. When Mom still yelled out each time she moved her cadera, I kept her home. By the time the sun had set, some liquid morphine had been delivered. I was instructed to give her a dose every hour until she was no longer in pain. After four doses, she paced the area between her bed and my desk, her steps sending out chispas.

"Where ees the letter fron Colombia?" she asked, looking at me through narrow, suspicious eyes.

My fear had grown too big for me to manage. I misplaced the acceptable lie, asserting instead that there was no letter, even phoning Susan to repeat the same thing, as if that would help. I strode back and forth with her, kicking myself for giving her so much morphine.

Locking the security gate at the top of the stairs, I caged us into a small, volatile space. Mom was in the bathroom squeezing the crinkly paper around a kalanchoe plant, saying she wanted some candy. Her hands pecked at the sound her mind identified as belonging to a candy wrapper. I tried to wrest it from her strong grip, all skin and bone and muscle.

"It's not candy, Mom," I said, my voice low and taut, "it's a plant."

"Don't yell at me, estúpida." She threw it in the trash and walked haltingly back to her bed.

I rescued the plantita and hid it in my room, like a child hides the bottle from her alcoholic parent. We went to our respective corners and fell into an uneasy sleep. I was startled awake by Mom's cry a few hours later.

"Linda!"

Jumping out of bed, I found her in the bathroom, clutching a blanket around her naked body. I calmly led her back to bed, chu-churreandola, slipped on her flannel nightie, tucked her in snugly, and stroked her forehead gently.

In the morning, I heard my mom mumbling in the bathroom. Walking in, she seemed caught in a mental warp. Instead of toilet paper, she was using her underwear. I tried wiping her with one hand while grabbing the dirty underwear from her claw-like grip. When the clean underwear dangled near her, she snatched it, soiling it as well.

Running for the phone, I called Eddy. "You have to come over, I can't do this alone. I can't do this."

I have no memory of how this scene resolved itself, but Mom ended up back in bed, comfortably snoozing. My brother arrived an hour later. I called Susan and told her Mom was not doing well. Susan was exhausted and we agreed she'd come Saturday after getting a good night's sleep. It was Friday; the same day of the week Susan had called me almost seven years ago to tell me Tot was not doing well. He was dead within four hours.

On Saturday, I left briefly for Teo's soccer game. Watching him chase down balls with such fervor interconnected living with dying, learning with forgetting, and filled my gas tank above the warning light. After the game, I picked up Susan, and by afternoon Mom couldn't chew anymore. We mashed a banana and placed it in her mouth anyway. The only medication we gave her was liquid morphine, and she went straight from toilet seat to diapers.

We called her familia en Colombia, letting them know the tide had turned and providing them the opportunity to say some last words with her. Her brother, sister, nieces, great-nephews, and good friends filled her soul with messages of love and cariño, though she barely moved or acknowledged their words. Michele dropped off supplies and kindly told us not to feed Mom unless she wanted it. Another letting go, to willfully stop feeding her.

On Sunday, Mom slept for most of the day, a few mumbles emitted at times. She was especially verbal when we disturbed her stupor to change her diapers, Susan wiping her while I gingerly took the soiled diaper and handed her a clean one.

"Brrruuutaaaass" slipped slowly from Mom's mouth. Her words were not very poetic, but they were definitely true to her.

I was filled with the need to make Colombian tamales, the only tradition from Colombia we practiced. I arranged the table with cut banana leaves and bowls full of capers, stuffed green olives, lightly steamed carrots slices, rice, pollo, salsa and string to tie it all up. The key was the masa, soft and pliable, soaked in a rich chicken broth.

My hands dove into the golden substance, closed into fists, and squeezed the clumps to smooth them out. Each spoonful spread onto the banana leaves was evenly moist with tomato and cilantro flecks amid the sea of warm masa. It was an altar of sorts, one of the few rituals my mom passed on to me. I had been refining the recipe she carried in her head for several years now.

After we steamed them for forty minutes, I put one on a plato and opened it slightly. The pungent meaty smell went with me up the stairs. Placing it on the table next to Mom's bed, the tamale bore witness to the first tamalada without my mom at my side.

We burned sage, its earthy aroma wafting with the yerbas we used to soothe Mom's body. Lit candles and flowers surrounded her with beauty, as she had always done in her home and garden. We called Eddy and told him to come back, as he had returned home to rest and tend to his two boys, one of whom was just eight months old. Like me, he needed to be there when Mom passed on, as we had not made it for Tot's death.

Peaceful music enveloped us as we held our vigil constantly, arranging shifts so everyone alternated sleeping and sitting. The candles burned unhurriedly, echoing Mom's slow breathing.

Susan kept busy with our mom's physical body, changing her diapers and swabbing out her mouth with pink sponges until it became raw and red. I couldn't stop her, my sister, who used activity to protect her tender spots, just like me and my tamale making. This caregiving was as intimate as my mother had ever let her be. Even though she said I should be glad I didn't see Tot gasp for his last breath, I still envied her for that intimacy. Kissing his cold, dead forehead did not compare.

On Tuesday night, a priest gave her the last rites. He spoke in English and Spanish, reminding us that hearing was the last sense to leave and to touch her with both our words and hands.

Wednesday morning, Michele came and checked her vital signs. All good and strong.

"I'll check back Friday."

Susan and I looked at each other as if to say: "That can't be. We can't do three more days." We reluctantly discussed Susan returning to LA so she could be available later in the week.

Later that morning, Tereza, a curandera, came to the house. I had begun having sessions with her a few months before, seeking support. The accumulated stress in the last few days had caused tensions to rise, and I hoped she could help my siblings and me. It was too complicated to sort through; we sat in the living room, uneasy but together. She burned copal and asked us each to focus on what we needed to do to say goodbye to Mom.

Susan cried, unable to speak.

"I like the smell of the copal," Eddy said.

Before Tereza left, she looked me in the eye and told me that it wouldn't be long. "You will know when the time is near." I shuddered, afraid I wouldn't know despite her confidence in me.

At about three-thirty p.m., I went to sit with Mom and hold her hand. "I will throw little papelitos to tease people," I told her. "I will put your favorite food on the altar for Día de los Muertos—aguacate, mango, tamales, café. These are my favorite foods too, Mamy."

She opened her eyes and looked right at me, her pupils dilated. The color drained out of her lips and she closed her eyes. It was time. The others came, circling her bed.

I held one hand, Eddy the other. Susan asked me to sing "Amazing Grace," a song suggested by Tereza for its high and low notes that joined earth and heaven.

> *"'Tis grace hath brought me safe thus far,*
> *and grace will lead me home."*

Her strong pulse slowed down and dissipated, her river of life departing.

And then I wept with ganas for my mamita. My sister held me and reminded me of all we had done for her. Eddy left and returned with a rose from my garden and placed it on her motionless chest. My children arrived and looked at their abuela, saw the flower, and ran outside. They went next door to our neighbors, telling them the news and asking for their small, pink roses, the ones Mom picked under the cover of dusk with her caregiver, Dalia.

Her nietitos climbed noisily up the stairs and laid the fragrant buds alongside Eddy's rose. Gina and her friend Anastasia stayed afterwards and played hide and seek, finding reasons to go hide near Mom, sneaking peeks to make sure she was really dead. At times, I did think she moved.

As I looked at my mom's body, I whispered too quietly for my kids to hear: *May you not miss me the way I miss my mother, with the terrible longing that comes from knowing she was not there with me, only for me. Missing her because I never had her in the attentive, sometime annoyingly loving fashion you have me. May you miss the fullness and richness of our relationship, not the shallow digging in hard ground frozen over with mistrust and no forgiveness.*

I couldn't bear all the years ahead without my mom. I went into my closet and pulled out the cloth doll she hand-sewed thirty years before and sat down on my bed.

Mom was the most inaccessible lover I had ever had— emotionally distant, unwilling to compromise, stubborn beyond words, and always needing to be right. How the hell did she and my dad last together without killing each other?

23.
An Extra Guest

THE SIX-HOUR TRIP TO LOS ANGELES IN A U-HAUL with mom's casket forced me to sit still for many hours. I absorbed the myriad of feelings that had been lining up outside my heart's door for the past six months. I looked in the side view mirror and saw the dark green van with Carolyn and the kids following us onto the freeway entrance.

A friend drove the U-Haul while I worked on the eulogy. It could not have been a more arduous six months, and every muscle in my body ached. Yet I felt full, llena de una dulzura I didn't think was possible. I pulled out my black laptop and the cassette player with earphones. The eulogy belonged to me, hands down. I had a taped interview with my mamita. Having survived twenty-three years and at least fifteen different addresses, its journey had reached an apex in this rented truck full of a most unusual cargo.

I did the math and realized that in 1981 she would have been a spry fifty-five, and I a young twenty-two-year old college student. While my voice was loud due to the microphone being too close to me, both my mom and I spoke awkwardly, as if practicing a foreign language with each other. We sounded like strangers. My Spanish was halting and I was nervous about asking personal questions in any language. My mother's voice was tentative except when she filled in the details of a funny story. There were quiet pauses, lots of laughter, and too many instances of me blowing my nose.

I was unutterably grateful for my mother's voice and spirit keeping me company on that highway we had all driven countless times. I listened carefully for those stories that illustrated her essence, as I did not want to simply chronicle her life biographically. It would be more of a memoir, more of a cuento. And it would be bilingual, just like the tape. De eso no tenía ninguna duda.

The hours flew by as I listened carefully, pecked at letters, and guessed at translations, all the while sensing her still body a few feet behind me. At times I burst out laughing, especially when she told the story of releasing the ranitas in science class to postpone a test. She helped get us through Buttonwillow, Kettleman City, and up the grapevine to Gorman, animando our sagging spirits for the days to come.

Our good fortune held until we hit the stretch of freeway from the San Fernando Valley into West Los Angeles. Damn, carajo y maldito sea. The plan to leave Mom at the mortuary just seven miles away disappeared below a myriad of red brake lights. It was Friday afternoon. I called Susan after hanging up with the mortuary.

"Hey Susan. We are going to have an extra guest tonight."

"Really? Who?"

"Would you believe Mom?"

"What happened?"

"El tráfico es horrible. I just think this is so Mom! She can't just die and be done with it. We're only three miles away. See you in an hour."

When we pulled into the driveway, Gina and Teo jumped out of the van and ran with glee to leap on Rafael and Steven. Fred and Miguel pulled up the back panel of the truck and started laughing.

"Oh my God. This is too much!" said Fred.

We all looked at each other and shared the same thought voiced by my nephew Rafael: "We can't leave her out here." As one, we climbed in to slide the casket out, spontaneous pallbearers carrying Mom into her home. We laid her down carefully in the living room and sat with her quietly.

Pasado mañana had finally arrived. She had willed herself to spend one last night in her casa. In the midst of our activity into the early morning hours to prepare for the funeral, Mom lay still, and yet her spirit swirled in and around us.

Soon, the sight of her casket no longer seemed unusual. In fact, it seemed perfectly natural.

24.
Wishes and Grand Schemes

AFTER MOM WAS BURIED IN HER CASKET ON TOP of Tot's, Miguel told us his sisters were willing to use their part of the inheritance to buy out our parents' four-plex. He had been renting a unit there for a couple of years.

"I am not so sure of this," Susan said.

"Me neither. It ties up their money for a long time without any payout," I replied. "Let's go to México and talk to them. I really don't want another brother-sister drama about money."

She stared at me like she did whenever I came up with my semi-loca ideas that involved her: three parts disbelief and one hesitant part that admitted I might have a point. We decided to take another journey with a purpose other than to recuperate from the grinding pace of the eight years since Tot had died. This was a chance to ask the questions we carried inside our hearts and see for ourselves their responses. Our itinerary had us departing with my kids the day after Christmas.

Christmas Eve found us in my parents' old house, where Susan and her family had been living for a year. I stayed in the kitchen helping Fred cook carne asada and arroz, unable to be the happy hermana at Miguel's surprise engagement celebration with Lola, his latest novia.

Out of the smallest corner of my compassion reservoir, I understood his life felt full of the possibility of love and financial security. Nevertheless, the victorious air that Miguel floated in did not mix with my grief. I had only recently erased mom-specific numbers from my cell phone and recycled the Alzheimer's caregiver card from my wallet. My bouts of loss still surged and I longed to drop anchor and rest.

After dinner, Miguel received a phone call from Tere. His voice rose octave by octave as he gestured back and forth with his hands. He signaled me over and we walked into Susan's bedroom.

"What is it?" I asked.

"Tere is sick. She can't go to Acapulco. I lost our connection."

We spent the next hour calling and never reached her. Miguel tried Victor and Arieti's cell phones and no one answered. With no way to reach Tere, Susan and I had a decision to make.

"Do we fly directly to Acapulco now or keep our original flight to México City?" Susan asked.

"If she doesn't go, then we can still meet Rosita and Joanna," I responded.

"I don't understand who is where, do you?"

"Nope. We are flying blind."

We flew into Acapulco with no idea where our sisters were or how to contact them. I fantasized that someone would be there to meet us, but the only greeting we received came from a taxi driver who dropped us off at a hotel. Exhausted, we tumbled into the two double beds, a twin snuggling with each of us.

At ten p.m., we were startled awake by a cacophony of disco music that vibrated our hotel walls and thumped on our frayed nerves. Our earplugs softened the pounding and kept sleep at bay until three a.m. when it ended abruptly. We woke slowly to the blessed quiet of the morning and waited, having left messages on the cell phones of my sisters and nieces with our hotel name.

The kids splashed in a pool full of Mexicanos on vacation and I joined them in the cool water. The day passed with no word, and we once again sought sleep amid the disco rumble for half of the night.

At lunch the next day, we watched the bungee jumpers across the busy carretera. The content smile on Teo's face was one I yearned for and sought with each visit to México. His eyes were open and happy, his smile wide and full of promise. Teo's hair was plastered to his head, the beautiful burnished brown of his antepasados, flecked with his gold highlights. Mi hijo was still skinny enough to have the slight outline of his ribs visible along his torso as he reached for his glass of Fanta.

Gina was busy spooning sopita into her mouth. A beaded braid hung down her face, kissing the tip of her eyebrow. The long, narrow fingers of her other hand played the tablecloth like a piano.

If they noticed our tension, they stored it inside the memory bank that is in every child's heart, only to be exhumed years later when sipping a sopa or reaching for a Fanta in the heat of a perfect summer day. Feeling a visceral imprint that goes beyond that day and transports them to Acapulco in December 2004.

❧

On day three I heard a shout and saw Arieti running toward us, with Tere and Rosita trailing behind.

"Tía!"

Arieti gave me a wholehearted hug and I felt my insides dissolve with relief. There was a flurry of hugs all around and we decided lunch in the hotel restaurant made perfect sense. Susan went down with our sisters while I took the kids to shower and change.

After ordering, I paused and soaked in our bravery despite all odds. My fatigue was a combination of insufficient sleep, apprehension about whether we would connect, concern over Tere's illness, and the time change. In spite of it all, we four sisters sat at the same table for the first time.

Tere looked as exhausted as I felt. "My pain is much better," she reported.

We did not speak of the death that had instigated this get-together as we drove to the north side of the bay after lunch. The kids were delighted to play with Gijo, the fuzzy white poodle they had met on their first visit to Tere's home. He was frisky, his little tail wagging at the sight of my cuates.

The ocean was on the warm side of cool, refreshing like a glass of agua fresca. My kids were never happier than when in the water with loved ones. In this case it was Arieti and Gijo. Gijo paddled around the shallow end while the kids jumped up and down a little further out with Arieti. I imagined Gina at twenty, her skinny frame filling out to a young woman's full bloom like Arieti. Gina's joy shone on her face as she dunked her head under the small waves, emerging like a brown-speckled seal to point her nose this way and that, alert eyes taking in the shimmer on the water as Gijo paddled toward her. She did not understand the pointed reasons that brought us to México time and time again, escarbando sorrow to see what good lay beneath the surface.

I was happy to sit next to Susan, my twin's beloved tía, even if she was more into the business of our trip than into the connection of las cuatro hermanas. We all had big energy and loud opinions that frazzled her by the end of the day.

Susan faced different levels of displacement with Miguel, Rosita, *and* me. She was the "eldest" in many unpleasant ways, until Miguel came and asserted older brother energy. She then met Rosita, and her position was further eroded with no added benefits. She had me, the second daughter who, like her, grasped for any morsel of love and attention from our parents. We even joked that I acted more like the big sister with my mandona ways.

On day four we finally had the conversation that had driven our decision to connect in person. It was hot and noisy near the pool. We left the kids with Arieti and Joanna and stepped into the air-conditioned room, seating ourselves on two beds, the northern sisters facing the southern ones.

"We want, more than anything," I said, "to know you are in total agreement with Miguel's plan about the inheritance."

"Sí, sí." Tere spoke decisively. "He explained it all to us and we agree."

"Are you sure?" Susan asked. "We can split the money and give it to you as soon as the estate is settled."

We wanted them to say yes, to go against their brother's wishes and grand schemes. We did not want any sisters to get screwed by any brother. We were sad and sorry about the male privilege that pervaded our family stories.

"No, we are fine," said Tere. "We support Miguel and don't want the money now."

"Yes," concurred Rosita. "Your mamá never accepted us and we never expected the money. If Miguel says this is best, we support him."

Susan cringed at the mention of our mom, while I breathed in the anger and breathed it out. It was still difficult, but less so than when I had first heard Tere's antagonism toward Tot during the first series of tough conversations. Susan told me later that when the comment about Mom not accepting them came up, she felt for the first time like she needed to take a side.

For her this situation wasn't about Mom—it was about our father and his choices. Susan felt protective of Mom, who was hurt by Tot's secrets even if she never voiced that. I didn't hear the judgment because I was too busy trying to find solutions to loosen our relationships. Or maybe I no longer believed that Mom didn't know.

Susan and I looked at each other and silently admitted defeat. Our older sisters were loyal for different reasons and we couldn't budge them. I got up and opened the door, ready to be with the generation who could learn from our pitfalls.

But first I wanted a picture of the four hermanas. It might be anticlimactic and somewhat staged, but I still needed it—a recuerdo of our connection. We were an archipelago of my father's seed, and our touch might not last beyond this trip. Walking outside into the bright sun, I waved Joanna over.

"Por favor. Pretty please, everyone behave."

We lined up, Rosita, me, Tere, and Susan, with no order at all. Not by most invested in our relationships, which would have me first and Susan last, and not by age, where I was the baby. Height was fairly irrelevant, with the range being five feet to five feet one and a half inches. The northern sisters were inter-spliced with the southern sisters. They all carried more weight from the past that I had escaped until I had made my first trip to meet my older sisters.

The next foto did not include Susan, who quickly stepped out of the montage. Rosita and I did not move from our stance on the left. Arieti, Teo, and Gina inserted themselves between Tere and me. Teo leaned in, a serious look on his face. Tere's hand grazed Gina's arms like a pianist poised above the black and white keys before a concert. She knew my kids were innocent but there was still an ancient caution. Arieti claimed us all, one hand stretching across my back so she could touch her tía Rosita and the other firmly holding her mother's arm. With her usual joyous smile, she also leaned down to touch Teo's head with her cheek and Gina with her chin.

Wanting something easy, I suggested we walk down to the ocean across the street instead of driving to the "better" beach. How bad can an Acapulco beach be? We reached the shore and settled underneath one of the multiple canvas umbrellas. The intense heat made me shed my red and white pareo, running with my kids into the blue, inviting water.

"What's this?" Gina pulled a plastic bag out of the mild surf.

Soon we were wading through soda can tops, plastic cartons, and general muck. I knew Tere and Arieti were on the beach, appropriately smiling like Cheshire cats. Next time, I would drive to a beach on the north side. We splashed around for a short while and emerged, feeling the hunger of many hours of effort.

Tere was leaning back in a relaxed posture on the lounge chair. "I was so nervous and now I can't remember why," she said.

The rise and fall of her laugh coaxed a smile from me. For the millionth time, I saw the warrior in her, surviving the doubts planted long ago about our right to be together and enjoy this meal of shrimp, rice, salad y cerveza.

We sat quietly and watched the kids running along the edge of the shore, trying to push each other in. They deserved the gift we were fashioning for them out of wounded hearts that beat for them beyond space and time and borders. We did not voice this or any decisions together. The legacy of retreating into our silos had not yet shifted.

Arriving at the airport two days later, we were ready to go home and sleep in our quiet beds and forget that disco music was ever invented. Approaching our gate, we discovered an avalanche of people. The kids and I grabbed a piece of the rug while Susan went to see about the delay.

"Security alert. They were told to fax all our names to the US so we can be checked," she told us. "We can't leave until they clear the list of passengers on our plane." After two hours, we boarded the plane and left México with our fragmented answers and worried hearts.

Part 5: Cracks

Colombian visit with my twins, my nephew Steven,
my two cousins Martha and Patricia, and my tía Lucrecia, 2004

Mom and Tot,
Great Buddha, Kotokuin Temple,
Kamakura, Japan, early 1990s

25.
Old Resentments Boil

H E WANTS TO MAKE DECISIONS HE CAN'T MAKE
yet! I am the executor and what happens is still my
responsibility."

Instead of calling me with news of her latest trials
with Mom, Susan now called about her constant dis-
agreements with Miguel over the emotionally intricate
and legally complex year and a half process of finalizing
our parents' estate. She hated having to manage Miguel's
premature claims to power. He had no patience for the
legal process or her designated role. Since it was going to
be his property, he couldn't understand why she refused
to let him make decisions until the title bore his name.

I asked Eddy to work directly with Miguel while I
walked a pencil-thin line of supporting both Susan and
Miguel on an emotional level; listening, pulling out possible places of agreement, desperate to save their tenuous
bond. Old resentments boiled inside both of them and
they appeared helpless to lower the heat.

Eddy was the perfect sibling to manage the sale. He
knew numbers and researched a fair price for the four-
plex, whereas I would have settled for less, more driven
by lingering guilt than he was. Just as he had tabulated
the multifaceted distribution of the overall inheritance,
he worked with all of us to focus on the process.

It had looked so noble initially, but the actual day-to-day chore of faxes and phone calls and emails felt anything but triumphant while my older siblings tore at each other's decisions. By the time the transfer of the four-plex wended its way to final signatures and a transfer of property, Susan was no longer speaking to Miguel or inviting him to family events. We had gone from calling him on some occasions, to including him all the time, to this heart-breaking impasse.

Because of my own ambivalent feelings, I had not visited with Miguel the last few times I was in LA. Despite years of effort to bring us together, I once again slipped on my blinders.

Instead, I planned a trip to Colombia with my chamacos and Steven. I would be moving into my mother's landscape without her, leaving behind the disheartening process of splitting my father's inheritance.

While having lunch on our second day, I conversed with my cousin Maria Elisa about my father's first family. I disliked guarding my words or making my familia in México invisible, spilling the news about the doble vida in the service of breaking the tradition of secretos.

"Did you know?" I asked.

"I had no idea. Rosendo was always well loved and gracious during his visits here. I do remember that la mamá de Rosendo told me about his other family when I lived with you." Maria Elisa said.

"¿De verdad? My abuela told you? Did you say anything to my mom?"

"No. She was my tía," said Maria Elisa. "I decided your abuela was trying to make things difficult, that she was lying. No se llevaron bien."

"That's true. They fought a lot," I agreed.

I had been right in guessing my dad's mom knew, and she chose to tell my cousin Maria Elisa. Was it to unburden herself? My abuela was very vocal in disagreeing with my mom so her reasoning was unclear to me.

One by one the four of us ended up in bed with a nasty virus. First Teo and Steven lay limp, dragging themselves to the bathroom and sipping sopa and té we brought them. Then Gina lay next to me drifting in and out of a fitful sleep. I was the last to fall, my dreams sliding in and out of my daytime fretting. Even though my parents had started out as adventurers seeking their own definition of freedom, they had eventually settled down. As I faintly saw Gina and Teo coming in to look at me and then heard the TV down the hall, I wondered what I expected of them, given my own crisscrossing journey.

On the plane home, Teo slept as he often did, strewn across his seat with his head in my lap. Gina diligently reviewed the emergency card and then opened up *Harry Potter and the Half-Blood Prince,* resting her head on my shoulder. I leaned my head toward her and said: "I miss my Mamy."

Gina looked up calmly, touched my leg with her slender fingers, and said: "Don't worry, you're becoming like her." She then turned back to read as I chuckled quietly at her sweet wisdom. My kids were breezes that cooled my hot, heavy heart. I closed my eyes and floated home.

26.
Triple Vida

FIVE YEARS HAD PASSED SINCE OUR HERMANAS visit in México and three years since I'd seen Miguel in person, though we had exchanged occasional phone calls. It was time to change that.

"I'm going to visit Miguel for a few hours," I told Susan during my next visit. She nodded calmly and kept on pruning my mom's roses in what was now her backyard.

Miguel agreed to me taping our conversation, as had Susan, Eddy, and Gloria in the previous months. His Spanish still rolled off his tongue like a skier down a steep descent.

We sat in his sparsely furnished home office, with a wooden desk, computer, and printer. I sat in his office chair and he pulled in a chair from the dining area. I could hear cars driving by from the open window.

"Did you ever ask our dad why he left you and your mom?" I said.

"I came here to ask him that, but the best I could do was to ask him: 'Why did you come here?'" Miguel paused, his mouth puckering. "His answer was that the pressure he felt from mis abuelos was too much. They were wealthy and didn't really need him. That was the most idiotic response I had ever heard in my life."

He clasped his hands, leaned back, and paused.

"Having money was not as important as having a father, especially when it meant leaving us alone. My tío Guillermo used to hit my mom and it killed me to watch. I would try to stop him and he would knock me aside. He could do this because we were the ones que no tenían papá to protect us." He rocked back and forth as he disclosed these memories, his eyes watering a few times.

My fingers typed as many words as I could keep up with; it was a story he was hungry to share. In the back of my mind I knew there was more than one reason Miguel left México, or he would have returned after getting this insufficient, disappointing answer from his father.

"Gloria told me she had asked my dad the question that burned in her: Why had he kept her under such a tight rein and been so distrustful of her? He told her she had misunderstood; he was protecting her from ending up pregnant, unmarried, and uneducated," I said.

Miguel sat forward as I finished. My comments about Gloria stirred something.

"Hay algo más," he said. "He didn't let anyone get close to him because of la triple vida he lived. Without looking for it, I found out about two women he had in apartments that he paid for. If you are living three lives, the last thing you want is for someone to get close to you and ask questions, because you are going to find out what is really going on."

I wanted to scream with disbelief. Instead I clamped down my feelings and said, "That's true." I tried to keep typing but my hands just lay on the keys of my laptop as my heart sank lower than it had throughout this entire journey of uncovering the truth about my father. I opened and closed my hands several times, hoping to get through the interview without showing Miguel the pain that was shredding my heart.

"I met Rosario at the hotel and had started dating her without knowing her connection to nuestro papá. She would stare at me and finally said I reminded her of someone. She asked me if Miguel was my only name and I said my name used to be Rosendo. She looked startled and told me I couldn't come back to the apartment because I might run into my father when he came to see her."

Miguel was left holding the biggest secret for many years. He wondered aloud, as I did silently, when did Tot live with us and when did he go to their LA apartments? She was young, Miguel said, early twenties to my father's mid-fifties.

"I never imagined my father could be with such a young woman," he said. *Me neither.*

Tot had helped her get a job at the hotel and he used this power to procure a lover. A time-honored tradition that left me choking on my loyalty, especially when I calculated I would have been about the same age as this mistress, with no idea of who came before her and who came after.

There was no way to soften this ugly secret. Tot's desgracia was like a beached whale—a bloated, smelly pile of rotting flesh. The room and Miguel became a backdrop, as my love fought back against a wave of disgust—how could Tot so thoroughly betray my mom, our family, and, in the end, the only person that mattered at that moment—me? I kept looking at Miguel, but I didn't care about his story anymore.

I did the only thing I could. I changed the topic. "You said you studied judo and karate so you could confront your tío?"

We talked for another hour or so but I couldn't concentrate anymore. My heart was distraught after learning my father was a mujeriego. I was glad I taped the conversation. There was no possibility of taking these shards and creating a pretty mosaic.

Numb and exhausted, I drove to Susan's for dinner. I should have parked my car and run to my sister, told her my heart was broken and sat together to wade through this new revelation.

Instead, I kept my mouth shut. My old defense mechanism—protect others by keeping it small and therefore manageable. Susan already had enough negative memories of Tot. Her strongest memory is of him working all the time. Even watching videos of him doing things with us was smothered by a fear she had as a little girl when he spanked her and my mom defended her.

His compadre Arturo had been unfaithful as well and knew about my father's first family. I wondered if they shared their stories about their wives and children and the women they had on the side? Arturo's wife Sharlene divorced him for his behavior. My mom stayed. She had to see that Tot and Arturo were best friends for a reason. My parents stayed in touch with Arturo's ex-wife Sharlene. What did Sharlene say to my parents about why she divorced him?

❧

I had loved watching my dad at the Century Plaza Hotel. Working in the coatroom on and off from my late teens to my mid-twenties, I checked coats at fancy events like the Golden Globe awards and at smaller affairs like a bar mitzvah celebration. If it was a big pachanga, I walked with my mom and Susan down the wide hallways and across the gilded reception area. We'd peek into the huge, chandeliered room to see the extravagant decorations on the main stage, and the hundreds of tables glittering with polished glasses and shiny silverware.

Tot would be walking briskly among the staff, giving directions and gesturing with his right hand, his eyes watching everything and everyone, anticipating needs and responding to guests cordially. Wearing his tuxedo and polished black shoes, he was a different person than at home, where he wore comfortable, old clothes and was a man of very few words. His hands did not look like that of a man who mowed his own grass and kept his yearly fava beans free from weeds. Tot's nails were clean, clipped, and shiny with clear nail polish. It was such a good performance that I believed he was genuinely interested in pleasing everyone.

I did my job well, too, darting up to receive a coat, handing a ticket to the patron, buzzing back to carefully hang it up, and then attending to the next customer. I marveled at the gowns that I usually only saw when we watched the Academy Awards on TV.

After the flurry of guests deposited minks of every color and style, we'd collapse into our chairs. My father didn't see any problem with his family working at one of the lowest rung in the hierarchy of hotel jobs—it solidified my impression that he did not overvalue material wealth or stature.

After we heard the clink of forks and knives surrounded by the low murmurs of hungry guests, a waiter would mysteriously appear with a large tray that held our dinners. We knew this was a stealth operation, as this was my dad's doing, and the head maître d' might not agree with us eating meals that patrons had paid upwards of one hundred dollars to enjoy.

I was always ready for the mad rush, grabbing tickets, handing over coats, watching the tip tray to make sure there were a few dollars to inspire generous giving and removing money when it got too full. As the night wore on, I reorganized the coats and racks for efficiency so we could all go home as soon as possible.

Did his women walk by when we worked in the cloakroom at the hotel, lingering at a pillar to watch us surreptitiously, the unsuspecting family who knew nothing about Tot's triple vida? Did they mock us for being tontas who thought he was a good man, a loyal man, oblivious to the truth that lurked behind every plush corner of the hotel?

If it was a big event, Tot would stand with his boss Frank, the maître d' for the hotel. Frank enjoyed teasing us in his Austrian accent, but I was uneasy around him. His house, I was sure, was bigger than our house, and his wife did not work in the coatroom. Even though he was Frank's right-hand man, Tot's comments at home indicated he thought Frank was arrogant, saying: "Frank es muy creído." This discomfort with Frank reached a climax maybe ten years later. Susan told me after the fact that Tot had been reamed out by Frank at a meeting of the waiters for favoring the Mexicans.

Tot quit on the spot, a rare breach of his even-handed work ethic. He was hired as a waiter at the International Hotel, where he had worked twenty-five years previously.

Tot arrived home exhausted from the physical labor and the humiliation of obeying a captain who knew less than him. A few weeks later, Frank apologized, and Tot returned.

We did not go to him for help much, as he and Mom had done their work too well. I remember being stuck in Heathrow Airport for three days waiting for a flight home. It never occurred to me to ask my parents to wire me money. They had not approved of my choice to take a gap year from Stanford, and I was not going to expose my lack of planning. Instead, I slept on benches and found others in the same situation so we could protect our belongings and share food.

About the time my father was screwing younger women, I was graduating from Stanford. During my first year as a sophomore transfer in a dorm, I would sneak in to the dining hall for breakfast, since my parents and I agreed to purchase the lunch and dinner only plan. That decision had a lot of holes in it. Por mi parte, I was caught in the struggle to be independent and abide by their thrifty example, never thinking Tot had a secret budget with women close to my age.

I followed my values of community, human dignity, and nonviolence, landing in the Catholic Worker social justice community on skid row in Los Angeles after graduation. Susan was pregnant by Fred, whom my parents didn't like, and Eddy had not signed up for the draft. My journal mentioned my mom had high blood pressure. I had thought then it was a consequence of not liking her children's life choices, but it could be that she had clues about my father's mistresses. The timing fit with what Miguel said about his discoveries.

My father may have gotten a sense of power from these relationships with younger women. Eddy told me Tot always had an inferiority complex I didn't see. He felt it came from Tot's early life, when he fought for everything and felt deprived.

Other than bandaging whatever wounds he carried, these women also required him to spend money that he siphoned away from our household. He received tips beyond his paycheck that he could easily have used to support his triple vida. Susan had questions about his money when he died and she had begun managing his accounts for Mom. He went through a lot of money— there was almost nothing left of it. Whatever his IRA had been, when he died there was only a few thousand left. He couldn't have had so little. She thought he spent it on his big screen TV and satellite. There were no records. Now I knew where at least some of it had gone.

To hide his triple vida from us would not have been hard, but for all this to occur under my mom's intuitive and suspicious nose? He thought he was cleverer than her, but he was not. It gave potential meaning to the lines in her writing I had found before she died: *"But you couldn't be lonely, you have a husband. But you couldn't be bruised, I didn't hit you that hard."*

I imagine this scene occurring in her mid-fifties, when everyone had left the house. Maybe she found a detail he could not explain away and she confronted him. He hit her. He, like all of us, tenía un genio; and while he rarely showed us his wrath, we knew it was there, a fissure in the ground of his psyche that could generate an earthquake if certain conditions festered. I remembered the story of him throwing the cookie jar in their kitchen and Mom gluing it back together. This story had shocked me: I didn't ask questions because I didn't want to know.

Tot had walked through the living room where I sat with my mom years before, the tape recorder between us on the couch. The plan had been to interview both of them. How did Tot and I resolve, without a word passing between us, that the interview with him would never happen and that I wouldn't, as Miguel had said, get close to him and ask questions about his past? I never continued my interview with my mom either. I stopped at the point when they were courting. At the point where she got pregnant. At the point where the lies would have been caught on tape, for she would never have shared her desgracia.

At his funeral, I had wondered what would happen if Rosita had come—never imagining that a previous mistress could have been sitting in one of the pews. Maybe his compadres never came to our house because they knew, and he needed to keep it as far away from us as possible. La triple vida. I would have been livid if it had come out when I was younger, my feminist flames burning their brightest, fueled by a more absolute truth than the relative truth I sought now.

Instead of Tot giving me his legal trust and power of attorney, I wished he had given his confession—told us his story and let us wade through this together. To know my tears and despair would not kill me nor destroy my father's goodness, even if the cumulative damage to those he promised to love and cherish was steep. What I know is that if I had needed him, been ill or in a dire situation, he would have moved heaven and earth to help me. In that way and in all he taught me over the years, both before and after his death, he was a wonderful father.

There are some rooms in the house of his life I love to sit in and some that are always cold and bare. He no longer has a hold on us; we no longer have to guard our tongues. Each bitter pill only needs to be swallowed once, but this last one did not want to go down. I thought knowing the truth was enough, but it wasn't. He said I could make the hard decisions, and the hardest was to forgive him again and again.

My mother's willingness to forgive Tot gave me a foothold to consider for myself. Their bond bled often but endured, like a half-severed tendon that leaves the thumb functional but without the subtle movements that used to be there. Despite her aversion to mothering, some of my mom's decision to stay with him were her three children. I understood this from my own experience of leaving and seeing my children's unhappiness.

&

When I look at pictures of them in their last years together, posing in front of the largest Buddha in the world or holding hands as they end one of their Mediterranean cruises, they are not faking their companionship.

I gave my parents so little credit for what they carved out as affection in a world that did everything to make them hurt themselves and each other. I too often framed my journey as a chance to do things differently than my parents, as if I am an enlightened being who knows so much more about life, and especially about love.

When I had interviewed Gloria about my parents, she asked me point blank: "¿Mijita, why did you decide to dig all this up?" I didn't answer. I had to know what happened when secrets were no longer secrets, when my life was at peace with the past—to know that redemption is sometimes a word with three syllables and sometimes it is so much more.

27.
No Options Left

I VISITED MIGUEL A FEW MONTHS AFTER HE HAD shared the intimacies of his life and my father's final desgracia, still ruminating on the threads that hung loose and tattered from the folds of my heart. He had remodeled the apartment over the years to create more space. Having spent money on the entire property, he had not recouped his investment.

"I didn't listen to nuestro papá or Eddy," Miguel said regretfully as we sat on the sofa.

He and Lola had a daughter now, Aranza, who was three years old. I had brought my twins to visit them, still committed to keeping a pulse going between our familias. They played with her as we talked. Lola sat nearby, mostly quiet.

"They told me to be thrifty, that apartments don't accrue the same value when you fix them up. Instead, I treated this like a house and spent money on high quality appliances and materials. Now that the market is down, I can't make a profit to get my money back."

"Why is this important now?" I asked, noting his use of the "my," his sense of ownership apart from our sisters. He had mentioned several times since buying the property how he had to explain to them why there was no profit to share.

"I have decided to go back to México."

I had never expected to hear that. He had given up so much to be here, had committed to making this property profitable so he could share the inheritance with our sisters Rosita and Tere. His daughter was born here. Miguel was like my father in that he spoke as if he had figured out all the angles and his success was guaranteed due to his determined efforts and charm.

"Why?" I asked, although I had heard him bemoan the need to sell his large demolition vehicles over the past year as the building economy collapsed. His income had been dwindling for years and his hustling had not produced money.

"I have no more options left."

What does a good man do when he believes he has no options left?

Miguel sold the four-plex and told us all there was no profit. My sister and I had no interest in celebrating that our premonitions were right.

A few months later Rosita called Susan to ask about the sale, and Susan directed her to a website that detailed property sales. According to this website, there was a profit from the original price. That does not take into account what Miguel spent over the years he owned it, but the price surprised me when I looked it up. It was not a number that matched his sorrowful lament. Even though I asked myself again and again what could be salvaged from each unearthed secret, I was left shaking my head at this ending.

&

As for the beginning, no one alive remembers the details of when Miguel first came to our house. Even Susan, who is an elephant for most memories, cannot recall the day's events. She agrees Miguel must have come to the house and that we must have been told he was coming. She knows she felt a deep disappointment in Tot.

Eddy doesn't remember many details either, although he does recall the initial emotional aftermath as well. He felt discomfort at being related to Miguel but not having any way to make the connection real. There was also more to it, he recalled. A lack of resonance permeated the meeting because of a different culture and personality.

Even Miguel didn't remember when I asked him. "Did he tell you we didn't know about the rest of your family?" I asked.

"Yes. He told me it would be difficult. I would have preferred he said he was happy and he wasn't going to introduce me. I wish he hadn't. That way you all wouldn't have had problems and neither would I."

"That is a huge lie," I replied, too angry to keep up our old pretenses. "Keeping secrets does *not* make life better."

He didn't respond, just kept repeating in different words that he would have been fine and just lived his life. When I drew Miguel back to the actual question of when he first met us, he remembered only sitting in a chair or helping to paint some kitchen cabinets. It was highly improbable that his first visit would be to paint cabinets. He didn't remember any introductions or any explanation about how he came to be our brother.

Knowing my family and having interviewed them, I parsed the scene together with what I knew about our routines. Given the impact on all of us, it would seem the least likely day to forget, and yet it remains buried in our psyches. That is true control, for Tot to orchestrate this meeting and then create an environment where it disappeared like the pebbles he taught us to skip across lakes, here and gone. The emotional memory did survive—overshadowing the external details.

That tells me it was indeed ground zero. We had our reasons for forgetting the doorbell. Or for the three of us forgetting that Tot told us of this visit ahead of time, this rock breaking the window of our house of respectability.

Miguel's decision to return to México was one he imagined happening many years before when he married his first wife. That straddling of two intentions, two countries, and two families is a fence so full of people it sags under the weight of our unmet desires. It grows longer and longer, far more expansive than the border of México and the United States, and traverses a variety of terrains, ranging from major urban areas to uninhabitable deserts.

I got nowhere trying to solve the past when it meant losing the joy of the present, of my existence, of my siblings' existence, and of my children's existence. I never thought of my father as charming, but he played that card until it was just a scrap of paper in his back pocket. It saved him long enough for the pulmonary fibrosis to kill him. He did not complain. He embraced his slow death so well we did not talk about him dying until he was dead.

At the end of my last visit with Miguel, I took pictures of us all on his couch. Me and my damn pictures. It was my way of knowing I didn't have to rely on memories, which had proved fickle too many times.

I gave my sobrina Aranza a long hug, not knowing when I would see her again, walked out the door, and raced my laughing children to our car.

Epilogue

TERE AND I ESCAPE THE MAYHEM OF MÉXICO CITY on a bus, arriving in Ixtapan de la Sal near noon. It is 2015, fourteen years since we first sat together and ripped the scab off our familia's wound. She walks us to her special hotel where the price is reasonable and there is a spa she enjoys next door. But first, we carry our suitcases to the second floor room.

"No, these bedspreads are not comfortable," she says upon sitting down on the edge of her bed. She calls the maid back, asking for new ones. I watch and wait, my overall tactic when with Tere. We have a dam of mistrust between us that I cannot name or destroy without her permission.

After a light lunch, we walk to the community bathhouse on an overcast, warm day, passing houses, hotels and businesses with tile roofs, and more people than cars. After paying a small fee, we are escorted into a dark cavernous room with small dressing rooms and mineral pools known for healing and relaxation.

Stepping into the aguas termales, we sink up to our necks just like the chiefs of the Aztec empire did many years before. After about fifteen minutes, we move to the room where the mud baths beckon, along with natural light that smooth the many shades of brown into a cacophony of desert colors. The crowd is quiet for a bunch of Mexicanos, lolling like seals in the small separate pools, eyes half-closed and heartbeats resting. We pick a less crowded pool and slather warm mud on our skin, feeling the sticky softness become part of our arms and face.

Leaving the bathhouse after a massage, we return to our room with the new bedspreads. They are indeed softer than the first ones and I inhale gratitude for Tere's insistence. Her light snoring fills me with envy, as naps are not my forte. I read, my eyes periodically closing for a few moments.

"Let me take you to the Marriott," Tere says when she awakens an hour later. We catch a cab up a small hill and walk through the high-ceiled entry hall and up marble stairs to Roberto's bar.

Settling in comfortable leather chairs, we face a view out of the floor to ceiling windows with a wide vista of the crystal blue pool and lowlands. When our drinks arrive, Tere raises her glass to toast with me. "A mi hermana."

I gasp inside. Chipping away for so many years at the secrets and stories about each other, I am not prepared for it toppling so easily. My hands grasp the cool glass and I look at Tere.

"A la vida," I respond, washing away her words in an attempt to swim back to the familiar détente we have practiced for over a decade.

She looks at me. Sets her glass down. Leans forward into my fear. "No," she says. "I said something important and personal and you answered with a broad generalization."

Tears pool in my eyes. She is right to call me out. I did leave the intimate moment she gave me, too accustomed to my armor. She is offering me what these trips and my patience sought—her willingness to be my sister, to dare together to see what happens when the dam is destroyed and the parched valley below can flourish.

I let out a big sigh and lean forward to hug her and her words. "Gracias."

We sit quietly, occasionally sipping our drinks and listening to the guitarist until he begins a song Tere loves. She unabashedly belts out the lyrics along with the performer as if the song will die if she does not sing it. I wish I knew the words to join in, but instead I am her audience of one.

"What do you want to do when we visit Rosita and Joanna in Cancún?" Tere says after the song ends and she has passed me the rest of her drink to finish.

Tere and me in Ixtapan de la Sal Marriott Hotel, 2015

She and I are deciding together what our legacy is apart from the one our parents left us. A fragile trust matters more than the rancor and regret that hobbled us for so many years.

The secrets we carry still swirl uncertainly around us. Who had it better? Who had it worse? These are old and increasingly irrelevant questions. The more important question is how do we grow love, gratitude, and compassion in a valley that knew so many years without water.

In Memoriam

Miguel Angel Manrique Durand
February 8, 1950–December 5, 2017

Acknowledgements

THERE IS NO SEPARATION. EVERY WORD WRITTEN, every tear shed, every edit has been a spiritual and community practice. Much of my writing has occurred in communities that inspired, challenged, and honored my voice. Homenaje especially to VONA and the many teachers and writers I met and meet who write to eliminate the "single story" of communities of color.

Homenaje to my spiritual teachers Sensei Ryūmon Gutíerrez Baldoquín and Tereza Iñiguez Flores for holding my heart and feet to the fire, making my writing and life a place of fierce intimacy.

Homenaje to my parents and ancestors for making the hard choices to survive and thrive, for giving me a camino despite the pain that laced your souls from historical oppression.

A special shout out to Associate Professor Emerita Sandra Drake, my first writing teacher at Stanford, who chose to read my story first in class. That act of affirmation lit the fire en mi alma. Homenaje to all my subsequent writing teachers, with special appreciation to Chris Abani, David Mura, Ana Castillo, liz gonzalez, Esmeralda Santiago, and Marita Golden.

Homenaje to my editorial consultants, Marcela Landres and Minal Hajratwala, and to my MFA advisors, Reiko Rahna Rizzuto and Mariana Romo-Carmona, who all offered me stellar direction and a high bar of excellence that guided my thirteen-year journey to publication.

Abrazos to my writing colegas who sat with me in community to get the writing and craft work to happen, with a special abrazo to Sunita Dhurandhar, Erika Martínez, Daisy Hernández, Maria Ramos-Chertok, Irma Herrera, André Salvage, Vickie Vértiz, and my SLAAM (Sociedad de Latinas, Asiáticas, y Afro-Americanas de La Mujería) writing group, who witnessed and helped this story grow from toddler to adolescent—Dorothy Lazard, Meeta Kaur, Miriam Ching Louie, and Sara Campos.

Mucho amor to Daniel Olivas for perfectly timed consejos.

Much appreciation to my two coaches Grace and Luis who kept me focused in the early years when death and discoveries came too fast for me to hold well. Deep bows to those who published excerpts from the book to allow its first breaths in the world: aaduna.org, somosenescrito. com, and *Chicken Soup for the Latino Soul.*

Mil gracias to E.L. Marker, WiDo Publishing, and their supportive, enthusiastic team, especially my editor Karen Gowen. You never doubted the power and beauty of this story. Your "yes" came after rejections from multiple agents, scores of publishers, no less than twenty-nine residencies, and several grants.

Besos to all my friends, too numerous to name, who have cheered me on, gifted me spaces to write, invited me to share parts of this cuento at events and schools, and attended my readings and performances.

Gratitud a toda mi familia for being willing to ask and answer difficult questions and dig into painful moments to find some measure of understanding and healing, especially my siblings, Susan, Tere, Rosita, Miguel, and Rosendo.

About the Author

LINDA GONZÁLEZ IS A LIFE COACH AND WRITER born in Los Ángeles who has called the San Francisco bay area home since 1988. She is still raising and being raised by her twins Gina y Teotli. Linda has published essays in numerous literary journals and books, loves appearing as a storyteller on stages big and small, and received her MFA in Creative Writing at Goddard College. Her avocation as a writer began as a Stanford undergraduate. You can read her writing and learn more about her

Author photo by Tina Perez

thriving coaching practice at www.lindagonzalez.net.